AF304758
UGAND
EQUATO
S N

Lonely planet

SECRET WONDERS
OF THE WORLD

385
EXTRAORDINARY PLACES
YOU NEVER KNEW EXISTED

42
ASIA

100
OCEANIA

244
SOUTH AMERICA & ANTARCTICA

296
PHOTO CREDITS & INDEX

☀ INTRODUCTION

What do neon-pink lakes, skull art and a chicken-shaped church all have in common? They're secret wonders – known to few, and all the more intriguing because they fly under the tourist radar.

Within these pages you'll find hundreds of places to spark your curiosity. Whether they're overshadowed by more famous sights, too bizarre to hit the big time or just thrillingly wild, these secret wonders have all escaped mass attention. Some are entirely out of reach – too remote or dangerous for even the most adventurous traveller. But whether or not you can visit, they all guard stories that deserve to be told.

Of course, the world's most famous wonders deserve their acclaim. It's not for nothing that millions of travellers traipse the art-clad corridors of the Vatican, or snorkel with glittering shoals at the Great Barrier Reef. But these stories are well told already – and they leave countless lesser-known marvels languishing in the shadows. What's more, our enthusiasm is harming these popular destinations: overtourism can blight the travel experience and, in many places, put immeasurable strain on fragile ecosystems.

That's why we've reached far and wide for this compendium of overlooked sights. Some are naturally occurring wonders, like Brazil's sparkling termite mounds (p270) and petrified lightning in the USA (p237). But many are created by human hands, from Mexico's underwater art by Jason deCaires Taylor (p242) to Lithuania's startling Hill of Crosses (p184). As the human race strives to accelerate efficiency and profitability, there is a delight to be found in wonders made not to chase success or increase the bottom line, but for the simple joy of inspiring others.

Not all of them will lift your spirits, though. At the opposite end of our spectrum of wonder are sights that can inspire awe and fear, and penetrate the darkest realms of human imagination – like Singapore's hell-themed Haw Par Villa (p48). But it's sites of history, not myth, that truly chill the blood – places like the devastated village of Oradour-sur-Glane (p179) and Ecuador's Wall of Tears (p262). A few will challenge you to see old ghost stories in a new light, like the misunderstood Winchester Mystery House in California (p218) and the all-too-human origins of vampire tales (p254).

With hundreds of places to choose from, we hope you'll find a surprise on every page... pick one at random and see where it takes you!

1: Sculptures cloaked in algae at underwater gallery MUSA, Mexico (p242); **2:** Jumbled wooden icons at Lithuania's Hill of Crosses (p184); **3:** A psychedelic dragon at Haw Par Villa, Singapore's hell theme park (p48); **4:** The romantic ruin of Whitby Abbey, England (p254)

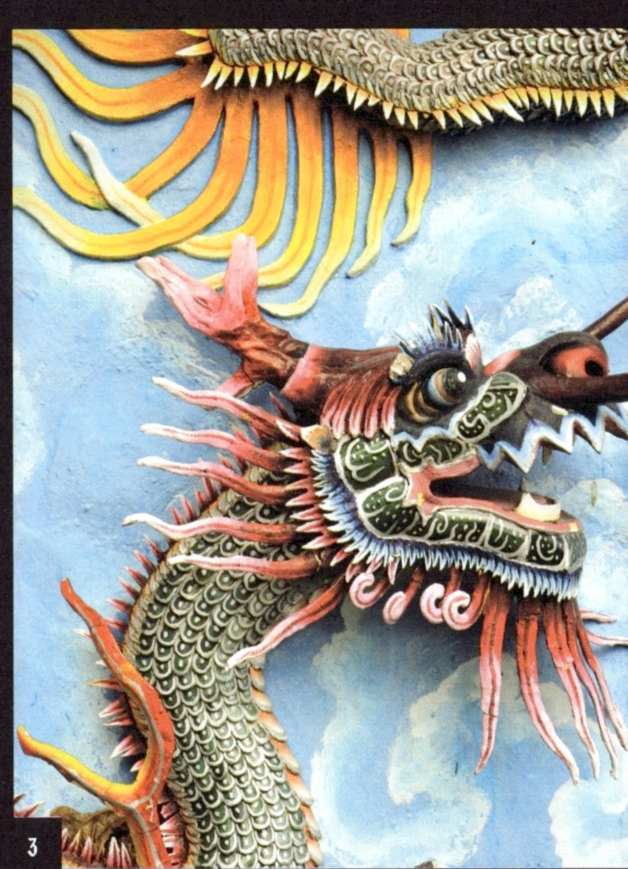

AFRICA & MIDDLE EAST

LEFT: Desert sands engulf an abandoned house in ghost town Kolmanskop, Namibia (p26)

THE LOST CITY OF HERAKLEION-THONIS

Shaken and then stirred, this city of antiquity – once ancient Egypt's gateway to the Western world – was toppled into the depths of the Mediterranean Sea by liquefaction and subsidence after a series of earthquakes. There it languished for well over a millennium, the swirling currents blanketing its countless treasures under layers of silt – until 2000, when the lost city of Herakleion-Thonis was unearthed in the Bay of Aboukir by French divers.

You may not recognise it by name, but you'll certainly be familiar with the legendary characters that form part of its history – Heracles is believed to have taken his first footsteps in Africa here, and Paris of Troy and Helen sought refuge in Herakleion-Thonis during their famous flight from Sparta.

While many priceless relics have been raised from the sea floor – such as 5m (16ft)-high statues of Egyptian gods, stele with pristine hieroglyphics and sections of impressive temples – less than 5% of the city has been excavated. Such was the scale of Herakleion-Thonis's sprawl (it was built atop muddy sandbanks and interlinking islands, much like Venice in Italy) that the underwater archaeologist credited with the find estimated it would take 200 years to fully exhume.

For non-archaeologist divers, the major sight in this vicinity is the wreck of *L'Orient*, Napoleon's flagship, which sank near here in 1798.

● **GET TO ABOUKIR** by flagging down an eastbound microbus along the Corniche in Alexandria. Make sure to review current travel advisories before planning a trip.

BANDIAGARA ESCARPMENT, MALI

CLIFF DWELLINGS OF THE DOGON PEOPLE

With tunnels, defensive towers and a mud mosque, Mali's Dogon Country may look as if it could be inhabited by hobbits, but these ingenious structures are designed for subterfuge and ambush. Built from rock and mud, these dwellings cling beehive-like to the sandstone cliffs and upper slopes of the Bandiagara Escarpment, the steep-walled cliff that closes off Dogon lands from the rest of Mali. Such isolation was very much the idea when they were built back in the 14th century, and remains a bulwark against invasion in more recent troubled decades. To spend days walking from one village to the next – marvelling at the elaborately carved doors, enjoying the playfulness of the conical straw-roofed granaries, sitting with the elders in the *togunas* (open-walled meeting places) – is to experience an unbroken line of history, from centuries-old settlements right up to the present day.

* **AT THE TIME** of writing, travel was not advised to Mali.

OSOGBO, NIGERIA

SACRED ÒṢUN ÒṢOGBO GROVES

Imagine wandering through a beautiful West African forest and stumbling upon incredible sculptures and shrines created by a renowned artist. The UNESCO-listed Sacred Òṣun Òṣogbo Groves are just that – a perfect fusion of old and new, nature and culture. Originally home to a shrine dedicated to the goddess Osun (the Yoruba deity of 'the waters of life' and fertility), the site was restored by Austrian artist Susanne Wenger in the early 1960s. She had arrived in Nigeria 10 years earlier and immersed herself in Yoruba religious traditions. Over the next five decades, Wenger and a group of Nigerian artists (now known as the New Sacred Art Movement) created numerous sculptures and other structures, all dedicated to Yoruba deities, such as Iya Moopo (the deity of all women's occupations).

* **THE GROVE IS** on the outskirts of Osogbo. Minibuses connect the town with Lagos (three hours). Make sure to review current travel advisories before planning a trip.

ANTOGO FISHING FRENZY

Fisherfolk can be a superstitious lot, but the good fishers of Koro in Mali surely win the prize. On a day chosen by the village elders in the dry season every year, the men of the village – a woman discovered the fish, legend holds, but women may not participate (go figure) – surround the shrinking lake. Six, seven, eight deep the fishers stand, jostling for position. Then, on the appointed signal, this concentrated mass of humanity storms the lake, each and every person hoping to grab a fish with their bare hands. The fish don't even stand a chance in this frenetic ritual that – on its serious side – reaffirms the local belief in ancestor worship.

AT THE TIME of writing, travel was not advised to Mali.

SENEGAMBIAN STONE CIRCLES

Death is confusing and mysterious, and so are these stone circles and burial mounds found across Senegal and the Gambia. Eerie and beautiful, sitting unobtrusively amid the region's grasslands, they consist of monolithic laterite pillars arranged in a circle around a burial plot, with one or more frontal stones to the east. Although there are a lot of them – about 17,000 spread across 33,000 sq km (12,740 sq miles) – and although they were made continuously for about 2000 years, surprisingly little is known about their origins.

Archaeologists aren't sure when the first circles were made or who made them. They don't know what the arrangements mean, how the burial practices functioned in the culture, or how they fit in with Islam, which arrived in the region during the height of stone-circle production. The burial style is a total conundrum: bones and skulls were arranged within the circles in elaborate patterns – a quasi-fence of bones set vertically in the earth, leg bones laid out in a design, a layer of jawbones covered with upside-down pots – and no one has any idea why. Oh, and locals say that stones occasionally light up at night. No big deal.

Maybe because of these mysteries (or maybe because it's a burial ground, where larger mysteries prevail), the fields of stones feel magical, as if they're a liminal place between worlds.

THE GAMBIA'S WASSU Stone Circles are the easiest to visit and have a museum on-site. Take a day trip from Janjanbureh, about 25km (16 miles) away; hotels can arrange tours.

DESERT CASTLES

The rock-carved city of Petra draws almost a million visitors every year, but it's by no means the only ancient complex rising from Jordan's desert sands. Best-known is the 8th-century pleasure palace of Qusayr Amra, 80km (50 miles) east of Amman. With one of the oldest bathhouses in the Islamic world, along with enduring traces of frescoes and still-standing defensive walls, it's an imagination-firing snapshot of the Islamic Umayyad Caliphate during their heyday.

Qasayr Amra is one of 30 or so palaces and stockades abandoned to the desert. Some 30km (19 miles) south of Amman, the ruined Qasr Al Mushatta is thought to have been a winter palace, never completed under the Umayyad Caliphate. Its sculptures long ago plundered, only walls and arches remain of its grand courtyard and halls – rely on your imagination to fill in the long-gone stonework with leafy and geometric designs.

● **A ROAD TRIP** from capital city Amman allows you to check out multiple sand-dusted wonders within a day. Going anticlockwise, head south to Qasr Al Mushatta, east to Qasr Al Tuba, then north and west to Qusayr Amra and Qasr Al Hallabat before returning to Amman. Make sure to review current travel advisories before planning a trip.

OWL HOUSE

In the unlikely setting of Nieu Bethesda, a secluded village in a remote corner of the Karoo semidesert, is a striking piece of outsider art – a surreal, poignant and at times disturbing work by the late Helen Martins. Back in her isolated hometown after a failed marriage, she set about filling her house and garden with hundreds of concrete figures, painted or decorated with colourful glass and wirework. I roamed the silent rows of camels, mermaids, farmers, nativity scenes and trademark owls, feeling saddened by the story of Martins, who took her own life in 1976, yet uplifted by her creativity in the face of bad fortune. *–JAMES BAINBRIDGE*

● **OPEN 9AM TO** 5pm daily. Get to Nieu Bethesda by car, or join a tour in Graaff-Reinet, 55km (34 miles) south.

GHOST SHIPS & WRECKS AROUND THE WORLD

Left behind or fallen into disuse, these rusty vessels are full of secrets waiting to be discovered.

SKELETON COAST, NAMIBIA

1. EDUARD BOHLEN

Almost 1000 ships are adrift in desert sands here, driven ashore by navigation-confounding fog and the relentless Benguela Current. One of the older ghosts is 95m-long (312ft) cargo vessel *Eduard Bohlen*, baking in the sun since 1909.

ISLE OF MAN, BRITISH CROWN DEPENDENCY

2. THE PASAGES

Stroll along Jurby Beach at low tide and come face-to-bow with the barnacled bones of a fishing boat. After foundering in a gale in 1931, the vessel's shattered hull lingers as a warning of this British Crown Dependency's sudden squalls.

3

4

7

10

GHOST SHIPS & WRECKS AROUND THE WORLD

OREGON, USA

3. PETER IREDALE

A skeletal four-mast cargo ship pokes through the ever-present sea fog at Fort Stevens State Park on Oregon's northernmost tip. The *Peter Iredale* lists wearily to one side and has graced hundreds of photographs since its sinking in 1906.

NEAR KARACHI, PAKISTAN

4. GADANI SHIP-BREAKING YARD

Innumerable whale-sized vessels have been dismantled into scrap at the now-dwindling ship-breaking site of Gadani. As workers' rights and environmental regulations improve, this cemetery of rusty ships may become one of South Asia's last.

SOMALILAND, SOMALIA

5. SHIPWRECKS OF BERBERA

A fleet, a swarm, a haunting? If there's a collective noun for 'shipwrecks' it surely applies to the rust-clad wreckage off Berbera. Numerous half-sunk ships flail along the shore, dating from the 1970s to the 2010s.

BEIRA, MOZAMBIQUE

6. MACUTI BEACH

The corroded wreck of a tugboat squats on the sand of Macuti Beach, right near the red-and-white candy-striped lighthouse. The boat is in semi-retirement; it serves as a breakwater on the beach.

PATREKSFJÖRÐUR, ICELAND

7. GARÐAR BA 64

After years of breaking through ice and battling storms, Iceland's oldest steel ship has found a picturesque place to rest – surrounded by basalt cliffs in a remote cleft of the Westfjords.

PEARL ISLANDS, PANAMA

8. SUB MARINE EXPLORER

Resembling a whale with big, baleful eyes, only the hole-punched hull remains of this 19th-century sub (and perhaps its disastrous track record of decompression sickness among crew who used it for pearl-diving).

GDYNIA, POLAND

9. GROM II

The twin *Grom* ships were British-built bulldogs of the sea: WWII's most powerful and well-armed destroyers. One lies submerged off the coast of Norway; the other stands proud in the port of Gdynia.

BIZERTE, TUNISIA

10. REMEL PLAGE

With salt-corroded iron studding the sand and wreckage listing in the surf, Remel Plage isn't a picture-postcard beach. But the rapidly decaying carcass of a Greek cargo ship has proved a hit attraction.

LUANDA, ANGOLA

PALÁCIO DE FERRO

Luanda's striking yellow Palácio de Ferro, operating as a cultural centre since 2016, is a beautiful building with a murky provenance. With its decorative iron balustrades and bold Art Nouveau parapets, it looks distinctly Eiffel-esque – indeed, popular legend suggests it was built for an exposition in France in the 1890s on the designs of Gustave Eiffel. Subsequently dismantled, it was put on a ship bound for Madagascar – but after the ship ran aground in storms off Angola's section of the Skeleton Coast, the building ended up in Luanda. Despite its romantic history, no official documentation of the 'iron palace' exists. Instead, it sits like an unsolved mystery amid Luanda's 21st-century oil towers.

• **THE PALÁCIO IS** in Luanda's city centre, known as the *baixa*. Opening times vary; entry is free. Make sure to review current travel advisories before planning a trip.

NEAR AGADEZ, NIGER

TREE OF TÉNÉRÉ

The last one standing. Almost. Once the sole tree in the middle of the Sahara – the survivor of the ancient Saharan forests – this acacia was justifiably famous. Not only was it the only tree in Africa featured on the Michelin map, but more importantly the Tree of Ténéré marked the location of a critical well, providing water to those crossing the heart of this inhospitable desert. That was until 1973, when it was knocked down by a Libyan truck driver. What were the odds of that? Today the tree is a metal replica, which stands in the original's place, to honour it.

• **AT THE TIME** of writing, travel was not advised to Niger.

KUBU ISLAND

Visiting Kubu Island is like stepping through the looking glass into an entirely different dimension. Rising from a remote corner of the world's largest network of salt flats – the Kalahari Desert's Makgadikgadi Pans, in northern Botswana – Kubu is a magical world of epic baobabs and horizons that never seem to end; a hallucinatory place where the sense of scale and singular beauty can be a dizzying experience.

But don't be fooled by the absence of water. Perhaps just five centuries ago, hippos wallowed in the shallows of what was once a vast inland sea (the word *kubu* means hippopotamus in the local Setswana language). More prosaically, the shorebirds of old bequeathed more than a mere name to this magical place – the white that stains the boulders overlooking the void is fossilised *guano* (bird poop), left by avian sentinels that rested here between fishing expeditions on what was once a real island. And as if to deepen the mystery, the island is also scattered with semicircular stone cairns, and archaeologists have discovered ancient stone tools left by peoples now vanished from the Earth. To find such unlikely connections to an otherwise forgotten past may seem incongruous – but when you sit with your back to a baobab and look out over the never-ending sweep of a world seemingly without end, time slips away into eternity.

● **THERE'S A BASIC** community-run campsite (kubuisland.com) on Kubu. Get here by 4WD with reliable GPS.

DANAKIL DEPRESSION

At the Danakil Depression, a volcanic rift in northern Ethiopia's Afar Region, the ground is literally coming apart at the seams – widening by 1cm to 2cm (0.4in to 0.8in) each year. The region's infernal navel is the Dallol cinder cone volcano: it's one of Earth's saltiest spots and, by average temperature, the hottest inhabited place on the planet.

This hellish landscape of acid springs and lava lakes is strangely picturesque. Magma boils the groundwater and sends it frothing up through the crater, dissolving the salts into an artist's palette of colours: yellow sulphur, vivid green salt deposits and Martian-brown rocks blur together like a neon parody of Monet's *Water Lilies*.

For scientists, studying Dallol's harsh conditions could unlock new insights into space travel. By understanding how polyextremophile microbes can thrive in this incendiary place, tolerating extremes of both heat and salinity, astrobiologists can investigate how humans, too, might survive in such intense conditions.

AT THE TIME of writing, travel was not advised to Ethiopia.

MATSIENG FOOTPRINTS

Where did human life begin? Legends of the Tswana people offer a surprisingly specific answer. According to oral traditions passed down by this Bantu-speaking group, who form the majority of Botswana's population, this rock-art site is one of four places where human life originated.

More than 100 carvings are engraved in the sandstone, a kind of 'we were here' graffiti that has transcended millennia. These faint footprint (and pawprint) designs were scored into the rock 10,000 years ago, showing where the one-legged giant Matsieng is said to have emerged, followed by his livestock and the tribes from whom we all descend. The legends aren't far off: scientists trace 100,000 years of human history back to Botswana (albeit further north, on the Zambezi's banks). Nearby, bright-green watering holes (former volcanic vents) are thought to have been used since the late Iron Age, and some locals still visit for ritual purposes – an unbroken line from the ancient past to present-day Botswana.

THE MATSIENG FOOTPRINTS are less than 45 minutes' drive northeast from Botswana's capital, Gaborone; part of the route is along a dirt track off the A1. Gaborone's National Museum & Art Gallery has information.

NAMIB DESERT HORSES

It's not often that you sit in a bleak desert waiting for a wild stallion or two. After all, desert-dwelling horses are a rare sight on this planet of ours. Yet that's exactly what I was doing at Garub Pan. To pass the time I considered the theories of their origin... Descendants of cavalry horses abandoned by the Schutztruppe (German Imperial Army) in 1915, or of steeds shipwrecked en route to Australia from Europe? Off-spring of the stud stock of Baron Captain Hans Heinrich von Wolf, who built Duwisib Castle 150km (93 miles) north of here in 1909? My thoughts were interrupted by dots appearing in the heat haze, and within minutes a dozen of the mystical horses paraded past me. Incredible. –MATT PHILLIPS

● **GARUB PAN IS** 1500m (0.9 miles) north of the road to Lüderitz in southern Namibia; the turnoff is 20km (12 miles) west of Aus.

BAT MIGRATION

Do you think Africa's greatest migration involves wildebeest plodding across the open plains of the Serengeti and Masai Mara? You're not alone. But some nine million more mammals are involved in this little-known migration in southern Africa each year. Between October and December, 10 million or so straw-coloured fruit bats descend into a tiny *mushitu* (swamp forest), within northern Zambia's Kasanka National Park. The concentration of life above you (whether flying or perched) is truly astonishing. Walk the forest floor beneath the hanging masses during daylight hours; come sunset and sunrise, climb into elevated canopy hides to join the massive bats as they take flight.

● **THERE ARE TWO** airstrips in the park for chartered light aircraft. If driving, it's 91km (57 miles) from Serenje.

LAC ROSE

Not far from Senegal's sprawling coastal capital, Lac Rose (Pink Lake) more than lives up to its name. On a hot, sun-drenched day in the dry season, this shimmering lake looks more like Martian landscape than West African countryside. Every inch of its mirrored, gently rippling surface seems to glow with a richly saturated pink – the kind of astounding, flamingo-like shade that nearly makes you doubt your own eyes.

The source of this pink pomposity is the lake's incredibly high salt content, which creates perfect conditions for a type of cyanobacteria known as Dunaliella salina to flourish. In order to better absorb sunlight, these microscopic salt feeders produce the red pigment that gives the water its vibrant, otherworldly hue. The landscape looks even more a figment of science fiction, given its surroundings: towering, blindingly white mounds of salt piled along the shore (the work of toiling labourers who make their living harvesting the salt), with rolling sand dunes just beyond that narrowly separating the lakeside from pounding Atlantic waves.

Much like in Jordan's Dead Sea or Utah's Great Salt Lake, swimmers can float effortlessly on Lac Rose's hypersaline waters. Those who prefer a less immersive experience can row out on a hired pirogue (wooden boat). Nearby guesthouses make fine settings for an overnight stay, and can arrange horse riding and other lakeside excursions.

LAC ROSE IS 30km (19 miles) northeast of Dakar, from where travel agencies can arrange day trips; you could also hire a car and driver. The best time to visit is from November to May.

EERIE NAMIBIA

• SHARED MINIBUSES AND long-distance buses are an inexpensive way to cover ground if you have more time than spending money. But renting a 4WD to self-drive around Namibia offers the freedom to reach far-flung sights, as well as comfort on the many gravel roads.

NAMIBIA

LÜDERITZ, NAMIB DESERT SOSSUSVLEI, SKELETON COAST

Spotting big game on safaris and taking hot-air balloon joyrides are popular ways to see Namibia's dreamy desert-scapes and teeming wildlife. But this southern African nation also has plenty to offer Gothic souls – from abandoned towns and blackened trees to the romantic wreckage along the Skeleton Coast.

EERIE NAMIBIA

KOLMANSKOP, *NEAR LÜDERITZ*

Some ghost towns remain frozen in time. Some rot unappealingly. Kolmanskop, on the other hand, is being spectacularly consumed by desert dunes, one grain of sand at a time. Built as Consolidated Diamond Mines' headquarters in the early 1900s, it hosted a bowling alley, a theatre and a casino. However, after richer pickings were found at Oranjemund, Kolmanskop's time was up – it was completely abandoned by 1956. Clamber over the dunes in the buildings' surreal interiors.

FAIRY CIRCLES, *NAMIB DESERT*

Radioactive soil, termites and plant toxins – they've all been considered as causes, but despite all the science, Namibia's fairy circles are still a mystery. Dotted randomly across the Namib Desert's eastern fringes (the NamibRand Nature Reserve and Marienfluss Valley are likely sites), these countless circular patches of 2m–15m (6.5–49ft) in diameter are devoid of any vegetation, their red soils standing out in a sea of golden grass. From the seat of a moving vehicle, you might just fail to notice this remarkable phenomenon, especially if you didn't know to look for it. But take to the sky (or your 4WD's roof) and the fairy circles leap out at you.

DEADULEI, *NEAR SOSSUSULEI*

Walk among the skeletons and shadows of an ancient forest in surreal surroundings at Namib-Naukluft National Park's Deadvlei, a bleached, cracked clay pan enveloped by towering dunes of bright orange hues.

ROCK ARCH SPITZKOPPE, *NAMIB DESERT*

Defying gravity for millennia and providing what is perhaps the best frame for a night sky in the whole world, the rock arch near the mighty 1728m (5669ft) massif of Namibia's Spitzkoppe is nature's gift to every photographer. The sky is so clear here that the stars are just as bright and numerous on the horizon as they are above you – call it a celestial blanket.

SINGING DUNES, *SKELETON COAST*

Sure, nature can inspire you to sing. But how do you feel about nature belting out a note or two itself? The unique mineral composition of the Namib Desert's sand, particularly in areas like remote Terrace Bay on the Skeleton Coast, ensures that it resonates (usually in notes E, F or G) when disturbed. Slide on your backside down a dune's leeward side and listen to it roar.

PREVIOUS PAGE: Desert sands fill an abandoned building in Kolmanskop **THIS PAGE:** An amber dune rises behind Deadvlei's camel thorn trees

GISHORA DRUM SANCTUARY

Clad in their national colours of green, white and red, Burundi's ceremonial drummers strike a jubilant beat at the Gishora Drum Sanctuary. Tightly coordinated rhythms have vibrated here for centuries, ever since Burundi's last independent leader pre-colonisation, Mwezi IV (1840–1908), established the sanctuary to commemorate his victory over a rebel chief. Drumming was the language of royal announcements, used to rhythmically herald events like coronations and festivals. The leading drummers are descendants of the Abanyigisaka (local religious leaders) and many of their treasured drums are originals, hand-crafted from animal skins and sacred hardwood linked to tree spirits and dating back to the 19th century.

● **AT THE TIME** of writing, travel was not advised to Burundi.

AL WUKAIR SCRAPYARD

The horizon shimmers as you drive south of Doha. Thousands of distant objects sparkle in the sunlight, like scales on a dragon's back – but as you drive closer you realise it's pure scrap: row upon row of wrecked vehicles gathering a soft veil of desert dust. The sight of more than 20,000 trucks and caravans is quite a contrast to Doha's palms, elegant archways and multistorey towers. The once-loved machines gloomily await their fate in the compactor; the flash of sunlight from mirrors and windshields is a final SOS.

● **LOOKING FOR A** postapocalyptic photoshoot location? You've found it. The scrapyard is 30km (19 miles) by road south of Doha.

KAYABWE, UGANDA

EQUATOR LINE CROSSING & RESTAURANT

Yes, you could have a memorable margherita in Naples or a saucy deep-dish in Chicago, but how about eating pizza in two different hemispheres at once?

The equator runs right through this simple restaurant in Kayabwe, Uganda. First, strike a pose in the circular equator monument – one foot in each hemisphere – then it's time for lunch. You're approximately 0.5% lighter at the equator than the Earth's poles, thanks to the lesser effects of gravity, so there's no need to hold back on finishing your final slice.

● **FIND THE MONUMENT** and restaurant on a drive along the Kampala–Masaka Hwy (80km/50 miles southwest of Uganda's capital, Kampala).

NGORONGORO DISTRICT, TANZANIA

LAKE NATRON

Hotter and saltier than the devil's armpit, temperatures at highly alkaline Lake Natron top 60°C (140°F). But conditions that are inhospitable for most life forms are heaven for some – such as cyanobacteria, and the 2.5 million flamingos who choose Lake Natron's crimson waters as a breeding ground. Rich in tasty spirulina algae and untouchable by their predators, the lake is a paradise for these blushing birds. A slated soda-ash mining project was threatened here in 2025, but local outcry saw it preserved for human and feathered communities alike.

● **AT THE TIME** of writing, travel was not advised to Tanzania.

FANTASY COFFINS

Dying to spend eternity inside an enormous beer bottle? Want your final resting place to be a large wooden chicken? Head down to Kane Kwei Coffins, a blink-and-you'll-miss-it workshop tucked away in a dusty corner of Accra, where a group of hardworking young artists create colourful fantasy coffins for the great and the good of Ghana – as well as for fans, collectors and galleries across the world. Dreamed up in the 1950s by carpenter Seth Kane Kwei, and continued today by his son and grandson, the coffins – known as abebuu adekai in the local Ga dialect – traditionally represent the lives, loves and aspirations of those that they carry to the grave. They were inspired by the litters, or okadi akpakai, once used to transport kings and chiefs; according to local stories, a chief that died before sitting inside his cocoa-pod-shaped litter was buried in it instead. Coffin designs have only grown more imaginative since: a giant pen for a writer, for example, or a guitar for a musician. More unique offerings have included a mobile phone, a hairdryer and even an ample bosom. If you fancy coff-in up the cash for one, you'll spend anything from US$1000 to several thousand. In 2014, a coffin in the shape of a Porsche made by a former Kane Kwei apprentice, Paa Joe, sold for a record US$9200 at London auction house Bonhams.

THE KANE KWEI workshop is situated in the district of Teshie, in eastern Accra; take a taxi from the city centre. Make sure to review current travel advisories before planning a trip.

GCWIHABA (DROTSKY'S) CAVE

Known only to the Indigenous San people until well into the 20th century, and reputed to be the hiding place for the fabulous treasure of picaresque 19th-century South African Hendrik Matthys van Zyl, Drotsky's Cave carries all the romance of the deliciously remote. The spot is known as Gcwihaba in the San tongue, meaning 'hyena's hole'. Hidden far from the nearest paved road in north-western Botswana, the cave is a cathedral of 10m (33ft)-long stalagmites and stalactites, not to mention bats with long wings and long ears. Most wonderfully of all, the sense of isolation, the silence and the complete absence of tourist infrastructure create a feeling that you've stumbled upon one of the Earth's last unknown corners.

● **THE ONLY WAY** to reach the cave is by 4WD expedition. Take food, water, maps and torches.

UNDERGROUND HOMES

Desert heat can feel oppressive, even inescapable. But desert dwellers in this small southern Tunisia town have found a way to hide out summertime temperatures that exceed 40°C (140°F): by burrowing their homes deep into the earth.

People in Matmata have built underground abodes, also known as troglodyte dwellings, for more than a millennium. Construction begins with deep circular pits, which serve as central courtyards. From there, passageways and rooms are chiselled into the rock, their walls are sealed with lime, and stairways are chipped out of the sandstone. The resulting living spaces are insulated from the heat and are typically 15°C (59°F) cooler than temperatures at the surface. Melding with the desert landscape, these dwellings are so evocative that one of them, the Hôtel Sidi Driss, won a starring role in multiple *Star Wars* films as Luke Skywalker's family homestead on the arid planet Tatooine.

● **AS WELL AS** Hôtel Sidi Driss, multiple troglodyte dwellings have been transformed into homestays and hotels. From Tunis, travel by train to Gabès, then board a shared taxi to Matmata. Make sure to review current travel advisories before planning a trip.

CITERNE PORTUGAISE

As I strolled in the condensed maze of crooked streets in the El Jadida's Cité Portugaise, I envisaged the scene 500 years ago when it was Mazagan, one of Portugal's first West African fortified colonies. However, it wasn't until I descended into the Citerne Portugaise that I felt like I'd travelled back in time. With nothing but a brilliant shaft of light from the outside world of today, I was left to absorb this late-Gothic architectural marvel. And how absorbing it was. The thin film of water in this vaulted cistern may have multiplied the light, shadows and columns by a factor of two, but it amplified its grandeur no end.

–MATT PHILLIPS

THERE ARE NUMEROUS daily buses and trains that connect the city of El Jadida with Casablanca.

OUTSTANDING OSSUARIES

Few sites are as deeply moving (or unsettling) as a room full of bones. These ossuaries are final resting places unlike any other: solemn and deeply evocative, and certainly not spaces you would want to enter alone at night.

ÉVORA, PORTUGAL

1. CAPELA DOS OSSOS

The remains of more than 5000 dead decorate the 19th-century 'Chapel of Bones' inside the Igreja de São Francisco – tapestries of knobbly vertebrae coat the walls, and femurs are arranged like ladders spiralling up stone pillars.

NEAR KUTNÁ HORA, CZECHIA

2. SEDLEC OSSUARY

Chandeliers, monstrances and coats of arms have been crafted from every bone in the human body at this creepy chapel. As a flourish, creator František Rint left a signature shaped out of tiny bones.

OUTSTANDING OSSUARIES

ROME, ITALY

3. CONVENTO DEI CAPPUCCINI

Hooded skeletons lean against a skull altar at this creepy chapel crypt. From the 1500s to 1900s, praying monks at this church and convent complex knew one day their bones would join those of their brethren.

DINGOLFING, GERMANY

4. SCHUSTERKAPELLE

In southern Bavaria, the charnel house within Dingolfing's Dreifaltigkeitskirche holds 60 delicately decorated skulls, adorned with calligraphy and botanical motifs designed to send loved ones to the great beyond with symbols of renewal and hope.

NEAR VALLADOLID, SPAIN

5. CHURCH OF SANTA MARÍA DE WAMBA

The mortal remains of half a millennium of Spanish monks are housed in the ossuary of this 12th-century church. Its walls are piled high with femurs, while 3000 skulls glare blankly at visitors.

KUDOWA-ZDRÓJ, POLAND

6. CHAPEL OF SKULLS

More than 3000 skulls of victims of cholera, the Black Death and numerous wars slumber inside the 18th-century Kaplica Czaszek in Czermna district. Another 20,000 bones are in the cellar beneath your feet.

LIMA, PERU

7. MONASTERIO DE SAN FRANCISCO

Beneath this pristine monastery's baroque towers reside the bones of 70,000 people. They're carefully arranged, radiating out from a cluster of crania.

VERDUN, FRANCE

8. OSSUAIRE DE DOUAUMONT

Inaugurated in 1932, this sombre ossuary holds the remains of approximately 130,000 unidentified French and German soldiers from WWI. Their bones lie in 52 mass graves, each corresponding to where they fell on the Verdun battlefields. Each engraved stone commemorates a missing soldier, while a touching collection of photographs shows scenes of survivors during the war and later in life.

HYTHE, ENGLAND

9. ST LEONARD'S CHURCH

This Norman-era church guards more than 1000 skulls and 8000 leg bones, the oldest from the 1300s. They're thought to be remains that were reinterred after local cemeteries filled to capacity.

SAINT CATHERINE, EGYPT

10. ST CATHERINE'S MONASTERY

Glowing gold in the desert sun, St Catherine's is one of the world's oldest monasteries. Former monks sleep peacefully in its small ossuary.

ROCK-HEWN CHURCHES

The churches of Lalibela are the worst-kept secret of a 12th-century king. Hoping to build places of worship that would be easy to hide from would-be Muslim invaders, King Lalibela ordered a novel manner of construction: straight down. The king's workers cut trenches deep into volcanic rock in central Ethiopia's highlands. Over 24 back-breaking years, they chiselled 11 churches – each from a single monolith – and scooped out tunnels to connect them.

Today, this rock-hewn 'New Jerusalem' is no secret. The entire site is UNESCO-listed for its unique architecture and astonishing scale, and it's a major pilgrimage place for Ethiopian Orthodox Christians who file into the red-rock churches to pray and to contemplate historic manuscripts and paintings of dragon-slaying saints. It's exactly what King Lalibela wanted: a close-to-home pilgrimage site that has outlasted the centuries.

Historians continue to marvel at how King Lalibela's workers sculpted the churches – particularly the cross-shaped Church of St George – with such precision, using primitive tools in the remote Ethiopian highlands. A solitary monk, Abu Gebre Meskel Tesema, set out to replicate the building process in 2010 by constructing Dagmawi Lalibela (the 'Second Lalibela'). Armed only with the type of hammers and chisels available several centuries ago, he has painstakingly begun excavating and carving a new site, 60km (37 miles) south... check back in a decade or two.

● **AT THE TIME** of writing, travel was not advised to Ethiopia.

GRANDE MOSQUÉE

Even on market Monday, when Djenné's dirt streets and squares are thronged with thousands of Malians and all their myriad wares, it's hard to take your eyes off the Grande Mosquée. Somehow both graceful and imposing, it rises above the dust like a living creature, with its porcupine-like wooden support spars jutting out from its fleshy mud facade. Constructed in 1907, and still the world's largest mud-brick structure, the Grande Mosquée is actually a faithful recreation of the mosque that was built here in 1280 after Koi Konboro – Djenné's 26th king – converted to Islam. The original stood for over 600 years as a symbol of the island city's cultural significance and wealth, only to fall into ruin in the early 1800s after the jihad of fundamentalist Islamic warrior-king, Cheikou Amadou.

Today's mosque, much like the original, requires annual maintenance to ensure its longevity, and every year at the end of rainy season, up to 4000 locals volunteer to assist the skilled masons from the Bozo ethnic group to complete the task. The structure's complicated wooden spine protrudes from the surface for this very reason – it is instrumental in allowing the craftspeople access during this re-rendering process. Non-Muslims are not allowed inside this place of worship, but great views of it are possible from the Petit Marché and the roofs of the nearby houses.

● **AT THE TIME** of writing, travel was not advised to Mali.

AYELABOLA

FÊTE DU VODOUN

Originating in Benin some 6000 years ago, vodou (or vodun) is an often-misunderstood religion that's practised in some form by more than half of the country. Meaning 'spirit' or 'deity' in the Fon language, 'vodou' is deeply rooted in its connections to ancestors and the belief that all animals, objects and places hold spiritual meaning.

Each year on 10 January, people descend on the coastal city of Ouidah for Fête du Vodoun (Vodoun Festival), an annual celebration of this rich and complex faith. Widely considered the spiritual centre of vodou, Ouidah pulses with energy as traditional rituals, music and dance fill the city – all in honour of vodou.

Among the festival's many highlights are the Egungun, masqueraded dancers that embody spirits of the deceased, thought to have returned to Earth to provide guidance or warnings for the living. With layers of colourful clothing, the impressive dress of the Egungun signifies their immense spiritual power. Emerging from the forest and moving through the streets during Fête du Vodoun, their procession culminates with a dance in the heart of the Ouidah.

FLY INTO COTONOU, the nearest major airport, and take a taxi or bus for 42km (26 miles) to Ouidah. Make sure to review current travel advisories before planning a trip to Benin.

THIS PAGE: A Sika deer in Nara, Japan (p69) basks in autumn's golden light

PLAIN OF JARS

Funeral urns, or convenient storage for rice wine? Historians hesitate over the meaning of these 2000-year-old granite and sandstone jars, some 3m (10ft) in height, scattered southwest of Phonsavan.

Archaeology is a daredevil pursuit in these meadows, which are strewn with landmines. Cluster bombs were dropped here in the 1960s, mainly by US forces during the Laotian Civil War, and unexploded submunitions are still studded in the soil. Picking carefully through this former warzone, archaeologists have been able to pin down the jars' age to around 500 BCE. They were initially thought to be brewing barrels for alcohol, while larger urns were found to contain tools, jewellery and bones, lending credence to the theory that at least some were funerary urns. They may have been used for 'primary burials', in which bodies are left to dry out before cremation; a cave nearby is thought to be the crematorium. Carvings of animals on the jar lids are not yet understood.

The region has 60 clusters of jars, and three of them have been completely cleared of landmines. Even so, it's important to stay on marked trails. Site One is the easiest to navigate and also the closest to the information centre. Sites Two and Three aren't as well maintained; independent travellers are best off visiting by motorbike or joining a guided tour.

BUSES CONNECT VIENTIANE with Phonsavan; from here, hire a bike or car, or take a guided tour. Make sure to review current travel advisories before planning a trip.

BAMIYAN PROVINCE, AFGHANISTAN

BAND-E AMIR LAKES

The six lakes of Band-e-Amir – Afghanistan's first national park – glow an unearthly sapphire hue. Local lore says the lakes were created by the Prophet Muhammad's son-in-law. The more prosaic explanation is that mineral-rich waters flowed through the hills, leaving deposits that gradually solidified into natural dams. Waterfalls babble between the terraces, and only a few paddleboats interrupt the lakes' pristine blue. War brought a halt to foreign tourism here, though a curious few do defy the travel warnings to admire this habitat of ibex, wolves and wild sheep, and to see the ruins of the Bamiyan Buddhas, 6th-century statues that were destroyed by the Taliban in 2001.

* **AT THE TIME** of writing, travel was not advised to Afghanistan.

CHAMOLI DISTRICT, INDIA

LAKE OF SKELETONS

High in the Himalayas, hundreds of skeletons poke from the shores of Roopkund. Human bones were first discovered here in 1942, igniting fears that they came from recent casualties – but the oldest date to the 7th century.

This glacial lake only reveals its bony inhabitants for part of the year. In winter, they're obscured by snowdrifts, but when the snow melts, hundreds of bones are on view. Folk songs describe a hail blizzard whipped up by Nanda Devi, the Himalayas' patron goddess, mirroring theories that these are the victims of a freak storm. Others have suggested a mass burial following a plague. A 2019 study aimed to settle the mystery: radiocarbon dating and DNA analysis revealed three groups of casualties from mass events in different time periods. Scientists found no evidence of a plague, but did observe bone fractures consistent with the hailstorm theory... perhaps the goddess' wrath is no mere cautionary tale.

* **ROCKFALLS AND HAZARDOUS** weather mean visiting remote Roopkund is near-impossible for all but extremely experienced high-altitude hikers in the company of local guides. Overnight stays in alpine areas were banned at the time of writing. Make sure to review current travel advisories before planning a trip.

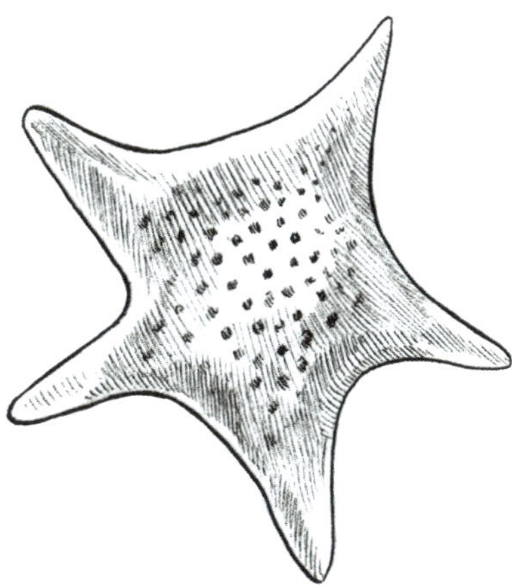

STAR-SAND BEACHES

Scoop up the sand of Iriomote Island's shores and you can hold entire constellations in your palm (if you look closely enough). Legends say that the star-shaped grains of sand on beaches around this tropical archipelago, closer to Taiwan than Japan's main islands, are the offspring of stars. In reality they are the prickly exoskeletons of tiny marine organisms, which amass in their millions on beaches along the northern coast of Iriomote. Starry sands are especially striking after storms churn up the seabed, washing more miniature fossils ashore. Sadly, some local souvenir sellers are depleting the beaches of their unique sand by bottling it for tourists – don't fuel the demand by buying any.

● **CATCH A FERRY** to Iriomote from Ishigaki Island, which is linked by flights from Tokyo.

LISONG HOT SPRINGS

The many fissures of Taiwan's mountainous terrain give rise to an abundance of natural springs unlike anywhere else on earth. Locals believe the waters are effective for everything from soothing strained muscles to conceiving.

For a wild impromptu dip, tread deep into Taiwan's lush mountains and valleys and find Lisong Hot Springs – a pristine wild oasis often hailed as the country's most beautiful hot springs. Secluded deep in a canyon, the springs are fed by waterfalls of warm water pouring down green-streaked walls, stained over time by calcium-carbonate deposits.

Naturally heated and amazingly clear, the pools are shallow in the dry season – ideal for lazy relaxation after the less than 2km (1 mile) day hike it takes to get there, which is mostly gentle but ends in a steep 70–80-degree sloping descent. Turn your visit into an overnight stay at one of the few camp-grounds that line the river.

● **PLAN YOUR VISIT** during the dry season, from November to March, when the water levels are lowest. Rushing waters during the rainy season can hide the pools and create dangerous conditions.

百年好合

PASIR PANJANG, SINGAPORE

HAW PAR VILLA

When Hercules made his journey to the underworld to dognap the demon pooch Cerberus, he had to wrestle ghosts and monsters. Visiting the underworld in Singapore was a little bit easier. All I had to do was jump off the Mass Rapid Transport train, stroll across Pasir Panjang Rd, and step into the bowels of hell...

Haw Par Villa, a sculpture garden created by eccentric brothers Aw Boon Haw and Aw Boon Par (best known for inventing Tiger balm), sprawls over 3800 sq metres (40,900 sq ft) of prime Singapore real estate. Coated in untold gallons of primary-colour gloss paint are more than a thousand statues of demons and deities from Chinese and Buddhist mythology. Many are arranged in gruesome dioramas of torture as a warning to anyone thinking of carrying out evil deeds in this lifetime.

I had encountered some wacky visions of the afterlife on my travels, but Haw Par Villa held a special appeal. Having been raised on Jimi Hendrix as well as Tom Wolfe's *The Electric Kool-Aid Acid Test,* seeing psychedelia in three living dimensions was much too alluring to resist.

Stepping through the innocent-looking Chinese gates, I was nevertheless unprepared for the nightmarish whimsy that was on display along the winding walkways. What was that? A crab with a man's head. And there? A girl with a snail's body. Nearby, the damned writhed in agony as they were crushed beneath grindstones and impaled on spikes, drenched in red-paint gore as if part of an early Hammer horror film.

Once little-visited and on the verge of closure, the park was given a makeover in the early 2020s to add modern comforts to the macabre atmosphere... including an air-conditioned 'Hell's Museum'. Certainly, it's not all doom and gloom. For every sword-wielding demon, there's an uplifting scene of Buddhist meditation or a magnificent Chinese dragon as large as a subway train. For the layperson, it's a mesmerising intro-duction to the rainbow world of Chinese and Buddhist mythology, and despite the patchy signage, the symbology – do bad deeds, get speared by devils – transcends the language divide. *–JOE BINDLOSS*

THE SCULPTURE PARK is open daily from 9am to 8pm. MRT trains run regularly to Haw Par Villa station.

ZHANGYE DANXIA NATIONAL GEOPARK

Bands of colour from vermilion to pale green cover a mountainous 500-sq-km (193-sq-mile) site in Gansu Province, where more than 20 million years of geological movement have pressed the sandstone into a multicoloured layer cake. Over centuries, the sandstone was weathered into pillars, while extreme desert temperatures split the rock to form creeks and cliff faces hundreds of metres high.

The name given to this kind of Martian landscape is *danxia*, and it can be found elsewhere in China, such as at the Binggou Danxia Park. This, too, is a landscape of towering rock columns and sheer cliffs – but its colours don't come close to matching those in Zhangye, where the hills blaze in shades of yellow and red.

Zhangye is threaded with walking trails and sightseeing cars trundle through, allowing access to lookout points over the spindly rock formations and tiger-striped hills. Most arresting is the 'Seven-Colour Mountain', which can be admired from the fourth and largest viewing platform (easily reached by the park's sightseeing cars). The hills flame scarlet and gold during sunrise and sunset, so photographers should rise early. A spot of rain also makes the colours of the rainbow hills pop, so time your visit for the wet-season months, between May and September.

● **TAKE A TRAIN** to Zhangye (30km/19 miles from the park's information centre) or fly via Xi'an.

GUMBEZ OF MANAS

A mausoleum covered in intricate terracotta tiles pays tribute to Kyrgyzstan's most legendary warrior. Tales of Manas' heroic battles and his unification of tribes have been passed down orally for centuries, gathering mythic embellishment along the way. By the 19th century, the stories were collected into the *Epic of Manas*; its descriptions of Manas' noble heritage and battles against the Afghans are still chanted at festivals today. Manas' highly ornamented tomb, commissioned by his wife, was labelled as the mausoleum of a young girl to prevent his enemies from plundering it. The ruse worked and his 11m (36ft)-high tomb, complete with elaborate Arabic inscriptions and a Kyrgyz-style dome, is still intact. A museum dedicated to Manas' life is nearby.

* **THE TOMB IS** about 20km (12 miles) east of Talas; drive there or catch a taxi from the centre of town.

HEAVEN LAKE

The caldera lake at the top of Mt Paekdu may look serene, but it has associations with both Loch Ness–esque monsters and North Korean dictators. The legend runs that Hwanung, the Lord of Heaven, descended onto the mountain in 2333 BC, and from here formed the nation of Choson – 'The Land of Morning Calm', or ancient Korea. Straddling the border between China and North Korea at an altitude of 2189m (7182ft), the crater lake is subject to persistent rumours about not one, but several watery beasts with long necks and horned heads. The 'Tianchi Lake Monsters' haven't been seen since some grainy footage emerged in 2007. But that's not to say that the lake has been silent: North Korea's state news agency declared that the lake's covering of winter ice cracked with grief when leader Kim Jong-Il died in 2011.

* **AT THE TIME** of writing, travel was not advised to North Korea.

TOMBS OF BAT

Prehistoric brick structures dot the deserts of northern Oman. The only snag with the so-called 'beehive tombs' is their lack of bodily remains.

Around 24km (15 miles) east of Ibri in northern Oman, chambers of carefully stacked bricks rise from the desert dust. They form a striking silhouette, almost mimicking the corrugated rock face of Jebel Misht (the 'Comb Mountain') behind them. For all the grandeur of their location, the Tombs of Bat look almost as though they could have been hurriedly assembled yesterday, so their true age – around 5000 years young – was overlooked for centuries. Only in the 1970s did archaeologists begin to investigate these mystery mounds in earnest.

UNESCO has praised the Tombs of Bat as the world's most complete 3rd-millennium-BCE settlements and necropolises – if indeed that's what they are. It's theorised that these were temporary tombs, intended to be used over and over again – which, combined with the passage of time, might explain why no traces of ancient bones have been found within.

This archaeological site covers a wide area. Bat has the largest number of beehives; Al Ayn, a further 30km (19-mile) drive, has some of the best-preserved examples.

● **YOU'LL NEED A** guide and driver, or a 4WD. From Ibri take Rte 9 to Ad Dreez, then east towards Bat.

KŌKOKU-JI

Want to spend eternity in a neon dreamscape? With torii gates and centuries-old gingko trees, Tokyo Prefecture's Kōkoku-ji looks like a traditional temple from the outside, but inside is a gently glowing columbarium where more than 2000 LED-lit glass buddhas line the walls. Each one corresponds to a shelf that holds someone's ashes; when friends and relatives arrive to pay their respects, instead of lighting incense they use a smart card to illuminate the statue linked to the resting place of their loved one.

● **THE CLOSEST SUBWAY** station to the temple grounds is Ushi-gome-yanagichō, 30 minutes from Tokyo's intercity rail station. The columbarium is the octagonal building.

HIGH-HEEL CHURCH

Looking like the glass slipper a giantess left behind at a ball, the High-Heel Church is a curious footnote to past epidemics. Composed from around 300 individual glass panes, the 17.8m-high (58ft) shoe-shaped building is a symbolic stand-in for the wedding shoes women weren't able to wear following an epidemic of blackfoot disease – a disfiguring vascular ailment with relatively high incidence among arsenic-exposed communities in Taiwan. The sapphire-bright building has won the title of world's largest high-heeled shoe-shaped structure; it's unclear how hotly contested the category is.

● **TAKE THE WEST** Coast Expressway 61 to the church from Xinying Bus Station. You'll be in good company, it's a popular spot to pose for photos.

PRINCESS OF HOPE

Hingol National Park, the largest in Pakistan, has sweeping deserts scattered with sandstone crags, all melting into an estuary of the Hingol River. But one sight impresses above the others: the Princess of Hope. It's difficult to believe that this regal rock figure was created purely by the chaotic forces of wind and rain. The naturally formed stone tower resembles a woman in a flowing dress and cap, her arms bent at the elbow. Befitting the Princess's stately silhouette, there's an A-list origin to her nickname: upon visiting the national park, Angelina Jolie was so inspired by the figure that she named her the 'Princess of Hope'.

 AT THE TIME of writing, travel was not advised to Pakistan.

LANTAU ISLAND, HONG KONG

BUFFALO BEACH

Go for a sunset stroll on the shore of Lantau Island, and you might attract the haughty stares of a feral buffalo – the beaches of this Hong Kong isle have become an unlikely spot for the bulky mammals to idle. Buffalo are a remnant of Lantau's agricultural past and a point of friction between would-be developers (who claim the cattle are a nuisance to traffic and tourists) and conservationists seeking to preserve the bovine population. Although development continues to encroach on the island's wetlands, the majority of Hong Kong's 180 or so feral buffalo can still be seen along the marshy shorelines of South Lantau.

 REACH THE ISLAND from central Hong Kong via the Tung Chung MTR line, or by ferry.

KBAL SPEAN

Fertility symbols are carved above and below the spray of a rushing waterway in Cambodia's Phnom Kulen, often referred to as the 'River of 1000 Lingas'. North of Siem Reap's world-famous Angkor Wat complex, this 150m (492ft) stretch of the Kbal Spean is lined with *lingas* (phallic symbols), along with carvings of the god Vishnu, monkey-headed Hanuman and numerous other Hindu deities. The setting is as exhilarating as the art, with waterfalls tumbling down mythic scenes: in one, Vishnu reclines with Lakshmi by his feet; in another, Brahma sits majestically on a lotus flower. Reaching the site requires you to wend through the forest, occasionally hanging on to branches and tree roots as you scramble uphill.

It is thought that hermits began sculpting in the riverbed during the 11th century, though some historians argue that the first *lingas* appeared 200 years earlier. The site was documented in 1969 by an ethnologist, Jean Boulbet, guided here by a local hermit. Cambodia's civil war prevented it from attracting much attention until the 1990s.

With overhanging trees and rushing water, it's all too easy to miss some of the most interesting carvings, so it's handy to go with a guide. Aim to visit between July and December, when water flows merrily over the rock.

● **KBAL SPEAN IS** 50km (31 miles) north of Siem Reap by road, then a slippery, uphill trek; wear hiking shoes. Make sure to review current travel advisories before planning a trip.

OLKHON ISLAND

'So this is Siberia?' I think to myself, as I lie on Olkhon's sun-warmed grass, gazing out across shimmering Lake Baikal. As I had discovered, Baikal's biggest island is a place that quickly dispels all the stereotypes of Siberia as a place of icy Slavic cruelty.

Olkhon is a must-see on the trans-Siberia trail, but it keeps its secrets remote – it's a dusty, seven-hour road trip from Irkutsk, eastern Siberia's de-facto capital. Wheezing buses spit travellers out in the tiny island capital of Khuzhir, a timber Soviet smudge and the only place to stay. This flyblown village is an unlikely spot for a backpacker hostel, but Nikita's Homestead is more than a dusty bunkhouse. This Siberian retreat is a village within a village, its cabins celebrating the region's shamanist traditions.

The island is a special place for both adventurous travellers and the local Buryats – ethnic Mongolians who inhabit Siberia's east. Eerie, peaceful and almost otherworldly, it's home to a horde of shamanist spirits but mostly uninhabited by humans. Dramatically barren in the south, Olkhon's north is a place of sandy-floored larch forest where the spirits dwell: the rocks, springs and oddly shaped trees are hung in colourful, wind-ragged cloth signifying an *oboo*, home of a benevolent spirit.

Recuperated from the long ride from Irkutsk, I take a minivan tour with a local Buryat guide. Paved roads peter out just metres from the village and we're soon treated to some extreme Siberian driving, our guide pounding an immortal Soviet-era 4WD van across the dunes. As we hang onto our pant-polished leatherette seats, we spot more *oboos*, the ground around them carpeted in kopeck coins. When we stop, our guide explains the spiritual significance of every rock, cliff and tree – all backed by Baikal vistas in shades of blue you never knew existed, with snowcapped mountains floating above the mist on the far shore. It's little wonder the Buryats chose this as the home for their pantheon of gods and spirits.

Dusted and road-weary, back in Khuzhir I find myself resting on that grass, listening to Siberia's silence – ethereal Olkhon, an unexpected island of exotic Asian tranquillity in Russia's vast expanse. –*MARC DI DUCA*

AT THE TIME of writing, travel was not advised to Russia.

AMAZING ASIAN FESTIVALS

Want to follow a phallic procession, watch grappling wrestlers or take part in a divine paint fight? Over centuries, countries throughout Asia have celebrated seasons, heavenly battles and artistic prowess through uproarious, radiant festivals.

BATU CAVES, MALAYSIA (JANUARY/FEBRUARY)

1. THAIPUSAM

Guaranteed to remain seared in your memory, Thaipusam is a full-moon event where processions of worshippers pierce and skewer their bodies in dedication to Hindu god Murugan.

DELHI, INDIA (MARCH)

2. HOLI

Want to celebrate spring with a rainbow-streaked battle? In homage to Krishna's penchant for pranks, devotees in India throw colourful dyes to honour the victory of good over evil. Delhi's celebrations are particularly wild; don't wear your best T-shirt.

3

4

6

10

AMAZING ASIAN FESTIVALS

KAWASAKI, JAPAN (APRIL)

3. KANAMARA MATSURI

Fancy watching penis-shaped altars carried aloft while eating suggestively shaped snacks? This phallic festival celebrates a folktale in which a woman vanquished the demon causing her *vagina dentata* (meaning 'toothed vagina') by breaking its teeth on a metal dildo. The festival has grown in popularity and now raises funds for HIV/AIDS prevention.

CEBU CITY, PHILIPPINES (JANUARY)

4. SINULOG

The Santo Niño dance – to a backdrop of hypnotic drumming – is the unmistakable hallmark of Cebu's glittering carnival, a pagan-turned-Christian festival dating back more than 500 years.

ULAANBAATAR, MONGOLIA (JULY)

5. NAADAM

Gasp at Mongolia's centuries-old military arts – wrestling, archery, horse-racing and spear-throwing – at this nomads' Olympics, held in midsummer with pomp, costumed parades and breathtaking skill.

HARBIN, CHINA (DECEMBER–FEBRUARY)

6. ICE SCULPTURE FESTIVAL

Palaces hewn from ice are illuminated against the sky, while snow sculptures of beasts and Buddhas are lined on the banks of the frozen Songhua River.

HUE, VIETNAM (APRIL/MAY/JUNE)

7. HUE FESTIVAL

Kite flying, boat racing and talent-shows unfurl next to traditional crafts such as calligraphy and dance at this biennial carnival of culture in Hue. Entertainment ranges from historic carnivals to high-tech light shows.

POKHARA, NEPAL (SEPTEMBER/OCTOBER)

8. DASHAIN

Fifteen intense days of ritual acts, from blessings to the symbolic chasing of demons, lead to a gory climax of animal slaughter. The spilled blood represents battles between good and evil.

YANGON, MYANMAR (USUALLY NOVEMBER)

9. TAZAUNGDAING FESTIVAL

The night sky blazes with floating lanterns for this full-moon festival marking the end of Myanmar's rainy season. At Shwedagon Paya, locals compete to weave monks' robes ahead of the festival.

BALI, INDONESIA (USUALLY MARCH)

10. NGRUPUK & NYEPI

The raucous festival of Ngrupuk summons processions of *ogoh-ogoh* (monster spirit sculptures) but the following day, all falls silent for Nyepi: Balinese new year. At this meditative afterparty, music is hushed, businesses close and locals contemplate the year ahead.

YUNNAN PROVINCE, CHINA

FUXIAN LAKE

After years of folk stories about a city under the water, the lichen-strewn remains of an ancient town were discovered in 2001 beneath China's third-deepest freshwater lake. First, divers detected flagstones and low walls furred with moss; soon archaeologists were mapping a site measuring 2.5 sq km (1 sq miles). Thanks to carbon dating, scientists pinpointed the age of the ruins to 260 CE, dashing hopes that the site could be a lost city of Yunnan's Dian Kingdom. Still, the truth is equally interesting: examination of carved stones found on the lake floor has revealed mystical images, including fertility symbols, ritual objects engraved with the sun and moon, and even animal-like masks.

• **ARCHAEOLOGICAL INVESTIGATIONS CONTINUE,** so you may be restricted to the lake shore.

GURVAN SAIKHAN NATIONAL PARK, MONGOLIA

YOLYN AM

In the middle of the Gobi Desert's 'Valley of Vultures', an ice field lies cocooned by a steep gorge. Thanks to the shade of this deep canyon in Gurvan Saikhan National Park, the ice of Yolyn Am sometimes lasts into the summer. In winter, the frosty mantle covers several kilometres. Layers of bluish ice, streaked with desert dust, create intricate natural sculptures as well as perilous crevasses; watch your step if you plan to hike the bed of the gorge. Tragically, the long-lasting ice field may soon be a fleeting memory, as locals report it getting thinner by the year.

• **YOU'LL NEED YOUR** own wheels (and robust ones at that) to reach Yolyn Am. By road, it's 45km (28 miles) west of Dalanzadgad, a thinly spread mining and tourist town. You can reach Dalanzadgad by bus from Ulaanbaatar.

HAENYEO

The women divers of Jeju-do are known as Korea's mermaids. Since the 18th century, the island's *haenyeo* (sea women) have been freediving to incredible depths to retrieve octopus, abalone and sea urchins, passing their skills from mother to daughter. For many years, the economic clout that came with their diving skills made them heads of their households. While the tradition is slowly fading, Jeju still has many women divers, some of whom are octogenarians.

Many *haenyeo* begin as children, scrabbling for seaweed in shallow waters before progressing to daring dives, ranking their skills by how deep they can go. Through years of experience, *haenyeo* train themselves to hold their breath for minutes at a time. For many, it's addictive; not just the rush of the dive and the thrill of seizing a catch with their own hands, but the economic independence that comes with it. The *haenyeo* divers have also become mournful observers of the effects of pollution on sea life, watching as the sea floor gradually empties of abalone.

Some locals still insist that male divers are too fragile to withstand cold waters, and that it would be scandalous for male and female divers to work together. While city jobs have lured many would-be *haenyeo* from the island, the Korean government still subsidises the diving equipment and healthcare of Jeju's mermaids.

● **JEJU-DO LIES OFF** Korea's southern coast. Numerous airlines fly to Jeju from Seoul and Busan.

HASHIMA

As the boat departs for the 'Ghost Island' of Hashima (nicknamed Gunkanjima), I'm finding it hard to stay calm. I keep scanning the horizon for the unmistakable ship-like silhouette that gives the place its nickname: Battleship Island. We leave Nagasaki's shoreline, passing barges and uninhabited islets, then someone calls: "There it is!" Sure enough, just like a naval warship, the island seems to float on the ocean's surface, blurry yet unmistakeable against the blue sky.

Hashima had been on my bucket list for years, first while living in Japan in the 1990s, then later again as photos of this wasteland cityscape began to surface in popular culture. Most famously, it served as the villain's lair in the 2012 James Bond film, *Skyfall*.

Ironically, Hashima was once the most densely populated place in Japan. However, after its coal mine closed in 1974, it was abandoned in just four months – its dormitories, equipment, schools, clinics and temples left behind like something from a postapocalyptic dream. Now walls have sloughed away, revealing forgotten dolls, TVs and kitchen appliances. Vine-choked alleyways are a riot of rubble-strewn artful decay. As we dock and clamber out onto walkways, I feel like I'm being escorted into a science-fiction world. Rusted iron spikes are twisted into clawlike fingers. The mineshaft seems like a gaping mouth. I blink and see ghosts of miners coming up from the depths, blackened from head to toe.

We stop a safe distance from the structures, in case of sudden collapses. The group has fallen silent, sombre. I imagine spending a night here, watching as the sun soaks the cement. It's impressively bleak, devoid of not just human life, but any life at all; I'm hard-pressed to spot even a seagull wheeling above. As we return to the boat, I think of the Inca, the Maya, the Anasazi, the Egyptian pharaohs. Will Tokyo, New York and Paris look like this someday? And will people visit, passing along marked paths and wondering who lived there, what caused everyone to leave, and where they went?

When the boat finally docks, the people around me seem more precious, and more fragile. It's a feeling that takes a long time to fade. *–RAY BARTLETT*

ACCESS IS ONLY via guided tour from Nagasaki's port; tours leave once or twice daily.

SAN JOAQUIN CHURCH

When colonising powers recede, relics of their former dominance linger like awkward interlopers at a dinner party. A throwback to Spain's three centuries of colonial rule over the Philippines, the Battle of Tétouan (1860) is carved in relief on the tympanum of San Joaquin Church, complete with soldiers on horseback and cocked rifles. This clash between Spanish and Moroccan forces – which took place 12,500km (7800 miles) from San Joaquin – secured Tétouan for the Spanish crown and prevented further attacks by Morocco on Spain's coastal towns. Dancing across the limestone and coral of this Roman Catholic parish church, the battle scene is an allegory for Christian colonisers triumphing over Muslim rule; some historians theorise that this imagery may have played well with 19th-century parishioners and their fears of Muslim pirates from Austronesia. The artwork showing the battle still has the power to draw gasps; Tétouan, meanwhile, is now once again part of Morocco.

● **DRIVE WEST FROM** Iloilo City along the coastal road to reach San Joaquin. Make sure to review current travel advisories before planning a trip.

BENEFICIAL MICROBES MUSEUM

No need to reach for the hand sanitiser. This Taiwanese museum intends to make visitors feel warm and fuzzy about bacteria, helping even germophobes to understand the microscopic organisms that inhabit our skin and guts. Visitors learn about a host of friendly microorganisms: there's *Lactobacillus johnsonii*, which helps humans to digest dairy; a suppressor of harmful bacteria named *Bifidobacterium longum*; and the bouncers of the bacteria world, the *viridans streptococci* group, which stand guard in human throats, preventing nastier microbes from entering. Expect fungus workshops, skincare experiments and educational games for kids. You'll leave giving a silent salute to the colonies fighting the good fight in your body.

● **THE MUSEUM IS** on Meizhou 1st Road in Yilan, 50km (31 miles) south of Taipei.

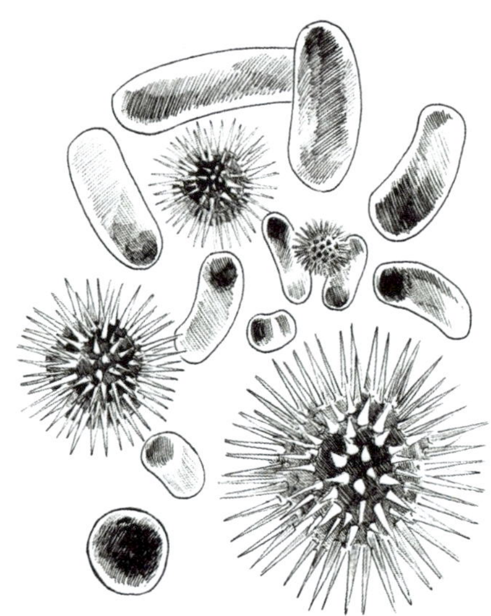

ESFAHAN, IRAN

PIGEON TOWERS

If you've ever defended a picnic from pestering pigeons, it might seem baffling that generations of Iranians built towers to attract flocks of these birds. But pigeon poop was big business in 17th-century Iran. It was used as fertiliser, and in an area such as Esfahan – where melon farming was widespread – enormous quantities of pigeon guano was required to keep dinner tables laden with fruit. To meet the huge demand, farmers needed pigeons to excrete en masse in a location where their nitrogen-rich droppings could be collected – without spilling a single, precious splatter.

The solution was to build huge dovecotes – towers designed for pigeons to land, rest and deposit their droppings. These brick towers resemble skyscrapers scaled to bird size, pitted with hundreds of pigeonholes and overlaid with plaster: a stylish, multistorey bathroom block. This innovation was not unique to Iran, though its pigeon towers might be the most impressive. There is evidence of industrial-scale dovecotes in ancient Egypt, and they endured for centuries in Scotland, France and the Baltics, and right across the Middle East.

Esfahan's stocky structures were so successful at gathering organic pigeon-processed fertiliser that thousands were built across the countryside. The availability of synthetic fertiliser led them to fall out of fashion; now they're simply roadside curiosities.

● **AT THE TIME** of writing, travel was not advised to Iran.

CAT ISLAND

As your boat glides towards Tashirojima's harbour, a furry welcoming crew stands on the dock. Dozens of cats – the dominant residents here – greet the arriving boats, mewling for food scraps and checking that no forbidden dogs make it ashore.

Cats outnumber humans by six to one on Tashirojima, and the ratio seems likely to increase in their favour, given the island's ageing population. Feline numbers swelled, thanks to enduring beliefs that cats bring good luck, and that fortune can be further cultivated by caring for them. Keeping them as pets is considered unseemly, so the kitty population roams freely on the island; perching on roofs, stalking through alleys, and making a lovable nuisance of themselves.

Tashirojima's two historic industries, silk and fishing, have ensured centuries of red-carpet treatment for felines. During the Edo period, cats were encouraged to chase mice away from silkworms, thereby safeguarding the source of the island's wealth. Later on, it was the fishing industry that cared for Tashirojima's cats. Fisherfolk became accustomed to the sight of cats begging for scraps of the day's catch. Soon, moggy mood swings were being interpreted in an attempt to predict weather at sea. Superstitious locals even consider cats to be lucky charms that protected the island from worse destruction during the 2011 tsunami.

CATCH A FERRY to the island from Ishinomaki in northern Honshū; it is best explored as a day trip.

JOHOR BAHRU, MALAYSIA

ARULMIGU SRI RAJAKALIAMMAN TEMPLE

Shield your eyes as you step into this sanctuary of twinkling beads and glass mosaics. A stray beam of light provided the inspiration for Malaysia's first and only glass temple: while pondering how to rebuild one of Johor Bahru's oldest temples, a ray of light struck the eyes of Guru Bhagawan Sittar. Learning that the light source was a reflection from a glass icon more than a mile away, Sittar was inspired to create a temple of glass to draw believers into its light. Inside, crystal chandeliers set beams bouncing off glass icons, and the walls are spangled with beads, each one engraved with a prayer. Most impressive is the multicoloured mosaic, made from more than 300,000 pieces of glass.

● **THE TEMPLE IS** 1km (0.6 miles) north of JB Sentral Station. Tourists are permitted to visit in the afternoon.

NARA, JAPAN

NARA DEER PARK

For thirteen centuries, the most prominent residents of Nara have been the wild Sika deer who roam the city freely. Legend says that in the 8th century, a mythical deity rode into town on a white deer, proclaiming himself protector of Heijō-kyō (as Nara was then called). Until the end of WWII, the deer were considered sacred, and they are now heralded as national treasures.

Around 1300 deer wander freely through stores, restaurants and homes in Nara. Be prepared for them to head-butt you to prompt you to feed them – they aggressively eat anything, including belts, purses and cameras; stick to offering the *shika senbei* (deer crackers) sold by vendors. Many deer have learned to bow when fed, and they are so used to humans, they will think nothing of coming right up to you to ask for a snack. This is Bambi with attitude.

● **NARA IS 375KM** (233 miles) south of Tokyo; the Nozomi bullet train makes the journey in 3½ hours.

MANDALAY–YANGON EXPRESSWAY

Compliments are in short supply when it comes to Myanmar (Burma)'s roads. Slicing north to south, the hurriedly-built Mandalay–Yangon Expressway cut travel times in half, but has design flaws that cause several accidents per day. Sometimes grimly nicknamed the 'Highway of Death', its roadside signs warn: 'Life is a Journey, Complete It'. Meanwhile in Myanmar's purpose-built capital, Naypyidaw, there are places where the boulevards stretch 20 lanes wide, like Yaza Htarni Rd. In this eerily underpopulated city, dozens of lanes are lucky to receive a steady trickle of cars and bikes. Locals murmur that the road was cleverly contrived: an aircraft could land on this broad expressway, should an antigovernment protest need dispersing in a hurry.

● **AT THE TIME** of writing, travel was not advised to Myanmar.

VALLEY OF GEYSERS

Stretching towards Japan, the Kamchatka Peninsula in Russia's far east is a place where the Earth's fuming fury is never far from the surface. Kamchatka's 6km/4-mile-long Valley of Geysers is fed by the 250°C (482°F) heat of the stratovolcano Kikhpinych, and more than 100 hot springs and geysers huff steam into the frigid air. But this basin in Kronotsky Nature Reserve is so far-flung that its geological marvels were only fully explored in the 1970s. One of the most chilling discoveries was the Valley of Death, a narrow 2km/1.2-mile-long creek where volcanic gases accumulate in such a high concentration that they kill animals and birds who stray too close.

● **AT THE TIME** of writing, travel was not advised to Russia.

TOWERS OF SILENCE

It has been generations since the last sky burial took place in Dakhmeh-ye Zartoshtiyun (the Towers of Silence) at Yazd in central Iran, but vultures still circle ominously overhead in the thermal currents. The modern age has scattered the traditions of Zoroastrianism – one of the world's most ancient religions – to the desert winds, but the hills around Yazd preserve traces of one of its most enigmatic customs. Rising from a silent plain, these eerie stone towers, known as *dakhmas*, were once alive with carrion feeders, as the dead were laid out in tidy rows and slowly picked clean beneath the cloudless skies.

The story of Yazd is the story of a vanished civilisation. Untold thousands of men, women and children passed into eternity in the *dakhmas* of Yazd while Islamic empires waxed and waned and the Zoroastrian community dwindled to just 0.03% of the Iranian population.

These days, all that remains here are the low stone houses where the dead were ritually bathed, the concentric circles where their bodies were laid out, and the central ossuaries where the bones were gathered. Combining Yazd with a visit to the Ateshkadeh fire temple in central Yazd – where a sacred flame has been burning since at least 470 CE – provides a tantalising glimpse into a culture that was old when Christianity and Islam were still young.

● **AT THE TIME** of writing, travel was not advised to Iran.

INTRIGUES & ODDITIES FROM BANGKOK TO CHIANG MAI

THAILAND

BANGKOK, KANCHANABURI & CHIANG MAI

Thailand's compelling wartime past and devilish theme parks offer an alternative to classic beaches-and-temples itineraries. On this trip around central and northern Thailand, architectural oddities and ghoulish histories take centre stage – it's still the 'Land of Smiles', but with the occasional rictus grin...

INTRIGUES & ODDITIES FROM BANGKOK TO CHIANG MAI

WAT SAM PHRAN, *NAKHON PATHOM, NEAR BANGKOK*

A scaly emerald dragon coils around the 80m/ 262ft-high tower of Wat Sam Phran, appearing to squeeze the life out of the temple. Go in through a turtle head, sneak past an elephant statue, then enter the dragon and spiral to the top; the journey represents the cycle of passing from joy to sorrow, heaven to hell. The temple is 40km (25 miles) west of central Bangkok.

KID MAI DEATH AWARENESS CAFE, *PHAYA THAI, BANGKOK*

Craving philosophical insights served with your ice-blended coffee? This thought-provoking cafe-exhibition challenges visitors to curl up in a womb-like chair, lie prone in a hospital bed, and then stay in a dark coffin for three minutes. It's designed to prompt reflection on the big questions (and maybe inspire some smart end-of-life planning).

HELLFIRE PASS, *SAI YOK, KANCHANABURI*

Built by a quarter of a million trafficked civilians and enslaved soldiers during WWII, the Thailand–Burma Railway cost more than 100,000 lives. Malnutrition was rife, diseases like malaria were rampant, and working conditions were brutal – especially at the treacherous section known as 'Hellfire Pass'. Contemplate the sombre history at Kanchanaburi's 'Bridge over the River Kwai' and nearby WWII Museum. The Hellfire Pass Interpretive Centre is 80km (50 miles) north.

WAT MAE KAET NOI, *SAN SAI, CHIANG MAI*

The nightmarish visions of *naraka* (Buddhist hell) at this theme park, 20km (12 miles) north of Chiang Mai, look like they belong on a death-metal album cover. Mannequins are speared and splattered with red paint, and 'fitting' punishments doled out in every diorama, from naughty schoolkids impaled by fishhooks to ghoulishly gynaecological torture for adulterers. Bring small change to light up the agonised sound effects and lighting (really).

ELEPHANT POOPOOPAPER PARK, *MAE RIM, CHIANG MAI*

We won't speculate on how this was discovered, but it turns out that elephant dung fibres are perfect for making paper! This crafting studio devoted to poo-derived paper tests the limits of sustainability and offers a vision for the next evolution of Chiang Mai's longstanding paper trade. Souvenirs are stink-free, and guided tours are available in English or Chinese if you book ahead.

PREVIOUS PAGE: A devil glares from Wat Mae Kaet Noi's garden of hell in Chiang Mai

THIS PAGE: Dragon-strangled Wat Sam Phran in Nakhon Pathom

SPIDER MARKET

Bugs for dinner? Okay, so they might not make it on to your weekly meal plan, but consider that entomophagy – the human use of insects as food – can be traced back to the earliest days of humankind. Many anthropologists believe that before the advent of agriculture, some 10,000 years ago, bugs were a staple feature in our diets. And in markets across Cambodia, diners can return to their roots – but this time, the crunchy critters are seasoned and deep-fried.

So what's on the menu? Insects, reptiles and just about any living thing that can be found underneath a rock. Larger critters, like snakes, sit drying in the sun. Some people offer even more exotic fare under the table or from the boot of their cars, such as bottles of so-called scorpion whisky that actually include the venomous creatures right there in the bottle.

At popular spots like Skuon Market (the town is known as 'Spiderville'), both locals and tourists line up at the stalls to ingest all manner of multi-legged, slithery critters. This outdoor market has been trading grains, veggies and fruits since the early 19th century. Over time, handicraft sellers also set up shop, along with chefs making ingenious use of insects: generous-sized bowls filled with crickets, moth larvae, water bugs and tarantulas. Granted, most diners prefer that their meals are not moving around on their plate, or looking them in the eye as they consume them, but for many foreign taste buds that is all part of the allure.

Most visitors treat the place like a walk-away cafe, grabbing a quick snack on the move. While some people prefer to eat their bugs *au naturel*, for those who prefer them cooked (which seems to be the majority), vats of boiling peanut oil stand ready to deliver a deep-fried, crispy-crunchy texture, as well as an extra layer of flavour. If you're not feeling it, other stalls will happily sell you bowls of steaming noodles. *–JAMES DORSEY*

SKUON MARKET IS 70km (44 miles) north of Phnom Penh (along NH-6) in the Cheung Prey district. Make sure to review current travel advisories before planning a trip.

KARYAMUKTI, INDONESIA

GUNUNG PADANG

These ancient stone columns occupy a serene location, scattered across a terrace in the fragrant hills of Cianjur – but they have ignited an archaeological controversy that continues to rage. There is little solid evidence that this megalithic site in West Java was left behind by a 20,000-year-old civilisation. But some geologists continue to claim that these hunks of volcanic rock crown a human-made pyramid – an idea popular with the Indonesian government, as it would herald the discovery of the most advanced civilisation ever known. Most academics are sceptical, suggesting that the site is a dormant volcano, and that its columns of rock probably date to 1200 BCE.

● **GUNUNG PADANG IS** a 24km (15 mile) drive southeast from Sukabumi. Make sure to review current travel advisories before planning a trip.

JIGOKUDANI, JAPAN

JIGOKUDANI HOT SPRINGS

We have 98% of our DNA in common with monkeys, so why shouldn't they share the very human joy of soaking in a hot bath? Jigokudani was named 'Hell Valley' because of its steaming springs and saw-edged cliffs. But there is nothing infernal about the sight of Japanese macaques (or 'snow monkeys') lolling in the naturally hot pools, particularly during the four months of the year when the valley is coated in snow. Japanese macaques are the most northerly primates in the world. Bathing isn't their only humanlike habit: scientists have seen them washing food before eating it, and even making snowballs.

● **THE PARK IS** open year-round, but bathing macaques are only guaranteed in winter. Buses run between Nagano rail station and the car park, a 30-minute walk from the springs. See en.jigokudani-yaenkoen.co.jp

SINGING DUNE

For those drawn to the enigmatic, the Singing Dune in Altyn-Emel National Park, 250km (155 miles) north of Almaty, offers an otherworldly symphony of nature's own making. With the right dry and windy conditions, the sand dune emits a powerful rumbling sound, not unlike an aircraft engine. This sound is produced when the grains of dry, pure quartz sand shift and rub against each other – whether it is when wind crosses over the dune or when a foot steps into it. The throaty grumble can usually be heard for miles around. But when it rains, no matter how windy it is, the dune stays completely silent.

● **ALTYN-EMEL NATIONAL PARK** can be reached from Basshi, located around 46km (29 miles) away.

YAMAL PERMAFROST CRATERS

Across northwestern Siberia's Yamal Peninsula, the ground is puckered with more than 20 craters – and they're grim footprints of human-made climate change. Haloed with debris and up to 50m (164ft) deep, the craters initially puzzled scientists. The jagged edges, surrounding debris and steep, smooth walls made it clear that these cavities were the result of violent explosions of ice and soil, as though firecrackers were suddenly igniting across Siberia.

Thanks to tectonic activity, the region is already highly volatile. But now, as warmer temperatures melt the frosty layers of soil, meltwater creates instability and releases trapped gases. This can result in explosions of methane that tear holes through the earth and release greenhouse gases into the atmosphere. It takes decades for these subterranean stresses to build up, so it's likely that many more geological pressure-cookers are simmering deep in the permafrost, getting ready to blow.

● **AT THE TIME** of writing, travel was not advised to Russia.

KARNI MATA TEMPLE

To be honest, I'm not an enthusiastic fan of rats. It could be the fleshy, hairless tails, or the times I've woken in dark, third-rate hotel rooms to find myself not entirely alone. But I can't claim I didn't know what I was getting into when visiting Bikaner's legendary rat temple.

Founded by priests from the Charan caste – a tribal people once worshipped as divine by Rajasthan's Rajput rulers – the Karni Mata Mandir at Deshnok is literally crawling with rats, but that's rather the idea. The scurrying, squealing rodents are worshipped by Hindu devotees as the reincarnated children of Karni Mata, patron deity of the royal families of Jodhpur and Bikaner.

From outside, this could be just another Rajasthani temple, built in the late-Mughal style by the 19th-century Maharajah of Bikaner. Inside, though, rodents rule. Everywhere, rats tumble over thresholds, skitter down handrails and wriggle through narrow nooks and crannies. In the inner sanctum, a living tide surges across the marble floor, scuttling between the feet of pilgrims to gather in hunched rows around giant metal trays of milk and *prasad* (ceremonial food).

Entering Karni Mata could be marketed as a form of immersion therapy for musophobes. For one thing, you have to go barefoot, so rats are definitely going to run across your feet at some point in the proceedings. Personally, I found this idea less alarming than the potential health risks of eating food 'blessed' by holy rodent nibbles. In the end, I braved a single piece of candy-style sweet *prasad*, reasoning that my immune system was sufficiently honed after several months of travel and that I could survive almost anything.

Perhaps the most striking thing about the temple, was not the swarming rodents, or the nerve-jangling sound of some 15,000 rats squealing in unison, but the adulation shown to the tiny animals by visiting pilgrims. On all sides, people were feeding rats choice morsels and even dishing out affectionate strokes and kisses.

This would be a nightmare to some, but to the faithful, these are *kabas* – 'little children' – and are treated as lovingly as human children in this family-obsessed society. *–JOE BINDLOSS*

THE KARNI MATA Temple is open daily from 4am to 10pm. Buses run regularly to Deshnok from Bikaner. Make sure to review current travel advisories before planning a trip.

SAGADA, PHILIPPINES

HANGING COFFINS

The hanging coffins of Sagada cradle their dead in a limbo between heaven and Earth. At this vertiginous, open-air cemetery in Luzon's mountainous north, coffins are strapped to the side of steep cliffs. Following the traditions of Indigenous Igorot peoples, the most honoured dead occupy higher parts of the cliff face, closer to the spirits of their ancestors. The tradition is practical, too: in hanging coffins, the dead are beyond reach of scavenging animals and floods. In past centuries, this burial rite was also a deterrent against rival tribes who might seek to grave-rob the heads of their enemies.

Igorot culture is at ease with the realities of death. Some people even fashion their own coffins, assisted by relatives if they are too frail. After death, a person's remains will be smoked, tightly wrapped in cloth, and carried to the cliffs.

Along the way, relatives and well-wishers flock to touch the shrouded body, which is believed to bestow wisdom and luck. Coffins are designed to be snug: bodies are put in a foetal position, so the deceased's departure from life echoes their birth. Bones are sometimes broken to squeeze the body into its final resting pose. Today, only elders follow these customs – but whether or not the practice endures, Sagada's hanging coffins are likely to loom over these misty valleys for many years to come.

● **SEE COFFINS IN** Echo Valley, a 30-minute hike (guides are mandatory) from Sagada's St Mary Church. Make sure to review current travel advisories before planning a trip.

WEEPING ROCKS

Toffee-coloured streams gush from a cliff face near Cimenyan in West Java. Curug Batu Templek's uncommon waterfalls are known as Indonesia's 'Weeping Rocks'. Their tears flow most abundantly between June and September, when the soil has been fed with plenty of rain; groundwater, rather than a river, is the source of these caramel cascades. Visitors come to bear witness to this sobbing cliff face (and sometimes to rock-climb between the cascading tears). The rocks are framed by thick forest north of Bandung, the main town of this volcanic region, and signs point the way across a colourful suspension bridge. Beyond the main Nasution Hwy (National Rte 1), roads are narrow, gravelly and not always suitable for some cars. Expect some surprised stares when you ask villagers for directions.

● **BY ROAD, THE** rocks lie 12km (7 miles) northeast of Bandung. Consider going by bike or motorbike, or hire a local guide. Make sure to review current travel advisories before planning a trip.

MY SON

Scattered beneath Cat's Tooth Mountain are the spellbinding ruins of the Kingdom of Champa. From the 4th to 13th centuries, this kingdom thrived along the coast of modern Vietnam. It's believed that monarchs were buried at My Son, where 18 temples still stand. Scenes from Hindu legends are visible, though tufts of grass now burst from the fired-brick walls; nature has been nibbling away at these ruins since their abandonment in 1832. The French rediscovered the site later in the 19th century, but the temples suffered badly during US bombings in 1969. Dodge the tour groups by arriving in the early morning, or in the midafternoon.

● **BY ROAD, THE** ruins of My Son are an hour west of Hoi An. Browse the on-site museum before you explore the temples.

DARVAZA GAS CRATERS

It's not easy getting to the Darvaza Gas Craters, which are set in a vast desert in one of the most isolated countries of the world – but, boy, when you get there you will certainly know about them. Seemingly an entrance to the underworld, one of the three artificial craters has been set ablaze and glows with an astonishing strength that's visible from miles away. For more than 50 years its boiling mud and blazing rock walls have created an intense, scorching heat. Now, finally, this giant desert furnace might be about to flame out.

The story goes that in 1971, Soviet engineers were looking for oil in the bleak Karakum Desert when their rig collapsed into a gas pocket below them. Fearful the methane would be dangerous, they set it alight, believing it would burn off in a couple of days. Instead, it raged for decades, repelling anyone who came near – except, strangely enough, spiders that continued to spin their webs close to the edge.

Roughly the size of an American football field and about 30m (98ft) deep, the crater was nicknamed the 'Door to Hell' by locals. The ferocity of the blaze and the enormity of its bleak surroundings make it an incredibly eerie spot, though in 2025 scientists announced that the fires were slowly starting to dim. It's best seen after sundown, when the daylight fades: the darkness amplifies the noise of the blazing gas and the sky is illuminated by its glow.

• **AN ORGANISED TOUR** to the crater is the easiest option; otherwise, take a shared taxi to Derweze, or walk for two hours across the desert.

ICE PHALLUS OF AMARNATH CAVE

At the Amarnath Holy Cave, situated 3888m (12,756ft) above sea level in northerly Jammu and Kashmir state, a subzero stalagmite draws Hindu pilgrims. This frosty protuberance is believed to be the symbolic *lingam* (phallus) of the god Shiva. It's a seasonal phenomenon: access to the 40m/131ft-high cave is nigh on impossible in winter, but in the late spring thaw, meltwater trickles into the cave and refreezes into the *lingam*.

Amarnath is believed to be where Shiva explained the universe's secrets to Parvati, goddess of love and fertility. But the ice *lingam* is shy around visitors; it melts more quickly when the body heat of groups of pilgrims raises the cave's temperature.

● **AT THE TIME** of writing, travel was not advised to Jammu and Kashmir.

AM PHU CAVE

Welcome to hell. This cavern carries a stern moral warning, allowing visitors to experience the Buddhist concepts of purgatory and punishment across 10 vivid levels. The gruesomely decorated chambers in this 302m/991ft-long cave certainly make a persuasive case for renouncing evil. Its pathways are deliberately disorienting, and visitors will find a spiritual scale where one's actions in this life are weighed. If that doesn't perturb you, maybe the fanged demons and dioramas of women and men being beaten bloody will do the trick. The hellish chambers are beneath Thuy Son, one of the so-called 'Marble Mountains'; the lofty crag rising above the cave represents the heavens. Clamber up a steep stairwell towards the light (how apt) to escape.

● **THUY SON IS** 15km (9 miles) north of Hoi An.

EXTRAORDINARY CREATURES (& WHERE THEY HIDE)

The Earth is home to a fascinating diversity of animals, some so extraordinary that it's hard to believe they truly exist.

INDONESIA, PAPUA NEW GUINEA & AUSTRALIA

1. CASSOWARY

Picture an emu with the fashion sense of a peacock and the temper of a prizefighting boxer. With powerful legs and razor-sharp claws, a single kick from these black-and-blue flightless birds can be fatal; back away slowly and admire their brightly coloured profiles from a distance.

CAMBODIA

2. IRAWADDY DOLPHIN

Cambodian legend says these blunt-nosed dolphins with gentle, sheepish smiles are the reincarnation of a woman who died by suicide after refusing an arranged marriage. Glimpse them from afar aboard Mekong River cruise boats from Kratié.

3
5
7
10

EXTRAORDINARY CREATURES (& WHERE THEY HIDE)

NAMIBIA
3. PANGOLIN

Somewhere between a tiny armoured tank and a dragon with a long, ant-slurping tongue, pangolins are increasingly rare. Try Namibia's Okonjima Lodge, nestled in a nature reserve also home to leopards, hyenas and more (though sightings are never guaranteed).

TROPICAL DEEP WATERS
4. VAMPIRE SQUID

This feisty little squid pulses through the deep-sea gloom, hoovering up marine snow (drifting organic matter) and surprising its enemies with a flick of its black cape – revealing fanglike spines on the inside.

TASMANIA, AUSTRALIA
5. PLATYPUS

With a duck bill, venomous spurs and a beaver-like body, this amphibious Australian icon is an adorable Frankenstein's monster. It's shy, but viewing points along Tasmania's Mersey River in Latrobe offer good chances of a dawn or dusk sighting.

THE CARIBBEAN
6. MANATEE

When Christopher Columbus clapped eyes on a 'mermaid', he was actually ogling a voluptuous manatee. These bovine ballerinas glide through the Caribbean's balmy waters, munching on seagrass and chirruping to one another.

ROTTNEST ISLAND, AUSTRALIA
7. QUOKKA

There's a furry welcoming committee of curious, dark-eyed marsupials on Rottnest Island. Spot quokkas scampering around Garden Lake and on the trail to Bickley Bay – just don't follow other visitors' cues (many people get too close and feed them).

GALÁPAGOS ISLANDS
8. FRIGATE BIRD

Literally wearing their heart on their sleeve, male frigate birds sport a scarlet pouch that puffs up when an attractive mate is in sight. Look up on a Galápagos cruise to see them soaring high, their iridescent black feathers catching the light.

PHILIPPINES
9. TARSIER

Don't be fooled by their bulging golden eyes that seem to implore, "who, me?" These elfin primates can jump 5m (16ft) and rotate their heads almost 180 degrees. Bohol's Philippine Tarsier and Wildlife Sanctuary is on a quest to save them.

BORNEO
10. PROBOSCIS MONKEY

Distinctive snouts give proboscis monkeys a mock-serious air. Females have sharp, upturned schnozzes; males sport wobbling, pendulous noses. Sanctuaries offer a chance to see them – but avoid places that encourage up-close photos.

LONGYOU CAVES

Generations of locals thought Longyou's ponds were bottomless, but something far more interesting was discovered after the waters were drained in 1992: 36 hand-carved caves. More than 30,000 sq metres (323,000ft) of grottoes have been revealed so far. Each chamber is roughly 30m (98ft) from floor to ceiling, and all are decorated with the same repetitive pattern of parallel lines, hand-chiselled in sandstone. Archaeologists' best guess is that the caves date to just before the Qin Dynasty, approximately 200 BCE, though no written record of their construction or meaning has yet been unearthed.

Five chambers have been opened for tourism, allowing visitors to marvel at symbols - fish, birds and animals - etched in the stone. Also puzzling is how the caves were constructed with such precision (some walls are barely 50cm/20in thick) and over what period of time. Scientists have estimated that 1 million cu metres (35 million cu feet) of stone would have been removed to hollow out the cave system. The pattern of parallel markings through-out would also have required an enormous amount of time.

One theory is that the Longyou Caves are an earthly recreation of the cosmos: the distribution of seven of its chambers have been compared to the formation of the Plough, part of the Ursa Major constellation. But many years are likely to pass before Longyou's secrets are revealed.

JINHUA, 55KM (34 miles) east of the caves, is an ideal springboard to visit Longyou.

MON STATE, MYANMAR (BURMA)

KYAIKTIYO PAGODA

A single strand of the Buddha's hair prevents this boulder toppling from its rocky ledge – or so the stories say. In any case, the 'Golden Rock' atop Mt Kyaiktiyo appears to defy gravity. This 7m/23ft-tall boulder leans towards the edge of its perch; confoundingly, only a small surface area appears to touch the bedrock, and even the destructive 2025 earthquake didn't shake it loose.

One of Myanmar's most sacred pilgrimage places, the entire surface of the boulder has been lovingly pasted with gold leaf, and a golden stupa (dome-shaped Buddhist shrine) crowns the top. Kyaiktiyo's shimmering coat is constantly being renewed. Buddhist pilgrims (male only) cross a bridge to the rock to daub their own glittering contribution on its surface; visiting three times in a single year is thought to be particularly auspicious. But the most enthralling time to visit is the pilgrimage season from November to March. A hypnotic atmosphere takes hold: candles are lit, devotees make offerings of fruit, and the chanting of monks vibrates through the night air.

Pilgrims remove their sandals before the challenging 11km (7 mile) trail from Kinpun to the rock. More casual visitors rely on a bone-rattling uphill journey by trucks, which set off when full of pilgrims. Visits at sunset are spectacular, but trucks heading downhill from the rock stop at sundown, so you may need to stay in a guesthouse near the pagoda.

✷ **AT THE TIME** of writing, travel was not advised to Myanmar.

BEIJING, CHINA

CHAIRMAN MAO MEMORIAL HALL

Few travellers dream of laying a marigold before the lifeless body of Chairman Mao. But despite dying in 1976, Mao Zedong still pulls crowds of visitors to his stately mausoleum in Beijing's Tian'anmen Square. The mausoleum is so high-security (bags and cameras aren't allowed) that it's almost like visiting a living head of state. Visitors file past flower stalls that overflow with marigolds, popular offerings to the founding father of modern China. Mao's embalmed body is behind glass, and visitors are ushered past so quickly that many wonder if it is truly the Communist leader's remains. Still, there's a range of Mao-themed souvenirs on sale, which last far longer than your fleeting glimpse.

● **CHAIRMAN MAO MEMORIAL** Hall is in Tian'anmen Square, walkable from Qianmen or Tian'anmen East Stations.

PANMUNJEOM, SOUTH KOREA

KOREAN DEMILITARIZED ZONE

A holiday on the edge of apocalypse might not be everyone's cup of Koryo (hangover-free ginseng liquor), but the 4km/2.5 mile-wide, 240km/149 mile-long buffer zone between North and South Korea is arguably the most famous sight on the whole Korean peninsula. And it has to be said, there's an undeniable frisson that comes from standing between gun-toting enemies surrounded by over a million landmines.

The place to come for a glimpse of Armageddon, and a peek across the razor wire into the secretive Democratic People's Republic of Korea, is Panmunjeom, the tense 'truce village' in the Joint Security Area. Access is only via organised tour; ripped jeans, casual sportswear and T-shirts with provocative slogans are banned.

● **MOST PEOPLE ARRANGE** tours in Seoul, just 55km (34 miles) from Panmunjeom.

IPOH, MALAYSIA

CAVE TEMPLES

Malaysia's famous Batu Caves draw almost two million annual visitors who pose next to gold-painted Lord Murugan and fend off kleptomaniac monkeys. But spectacular lesser-known temples roost in limestone hills southeast of Ipoh. Rocky stairs and walkways lead you to a shock of colour: Sam Poh Tong's pagoda, bright as a red hibiscus against a backdrop of limestone cliffs. A little further south-east, Kek Look Tong has a yawning cavern hung with chandelier-like stalactites, its gardens serene with Buddha statues and koi-filled ponds.

Snoozing on a hill north of Ipoh, Perak Tong was discovered and developed in 1926. The reward for panting your way up its 450 steps is the sight of a burnished 12m/39ft-tall Buddha, seated on a lotus blossom, who smiles out at cave walls adorned with serpents and Chinese calligraphy. From the highest point there are dreamy views across Ipoh to the hills; go early to experience it in blissful quiet.

● **DAILY INTERCITY BUSES** from Kuala Lumpur's KL Sentral Station reach Ipoh in about three hours. Make sure to review current travel advisories before planning a trip.

MANGYSTAU, KAZAKHSTAN

VALLEY OF STONE BALLS

Thousands of globes of sedimentary rock are scattered across the remote highlands of southwestern Kazakhstan, as though ancient gods played a game of desert bowls and left their playthings behind. This is Torysh, the 'Valley of Balls', and its signature spheres began to take shape 60 million years ago on the ocean floor.

There's no rushing the process, which is known as 'concretion': a mineral cement forms, gluing together everything from rock fragments to ancient fossils, layer by layer. Over time the rocks surrounding these bundles of tightly-packed debris erodes away to release the balls to the smoothing action of wind and rain, buffing them into spherical shape. Though they're little studied, every globe is a compact parcel of clues about the land's ancient past.

● **TORYSH IS 110KM** (68 miles) by road from Aktau, but the last few kilometres require a 4WD. Local tour operators include it in one-day tours of other geological marvels in the region.

BUKIT RHEMA

As a universal symbol of peace, the dove is a fitting emblem for a place of worship. But the grand designs of Daniel Alamsjah didn't initially turn out quite as egg-cellently as he intended.

Alamsjah felt a divine calling to build a dove-shaped house of prayer for all faiths, roosting in central Java's Magelang hills. Construction was a decades-long labour of love, but the final design fell somewhat short of a graceful dove: the hall's tower, shaped like a bird's head, has a gaping orange beak; its crown resembles a cock's comb. Affectionately dubbed Gereja Ayam – the 'Chicken Church' – it operated successfully as a multifaith place of worship, and Alamsjah also constructed a drug rehabilitation centre nearby. But costs began to spiral, and the main building was left unfinished. Over the ensuing years, its astonishing architecture and state of dilapidation drew in a steady stream of urban explorers.

Bukit Rhema has since been redeveloped as a seven-storey spiritual site, complete with prayer rooms and a cafe serving such delights as spicy fried cassava. Floor by floor, the complex aims to educate visitors about humankind's spiritual journey and inspire them along a spiritual path – and views from the Chicken Church's feathery crown, overlooking a forest canopy that trembles in the breeze, are poultry in motion indeed.

* **BY ROAD, BUKIT** Rhema is 20km (12 miles) south of Magelang town. The site has been developing various enticements to visit, from drawing lessons to nature experiences; check in advance to see what's on offer. Make sure to review current travel advisories before planning a trip.

ZHENGBEI TOWER

In the mountain village of Xizhazi, an unremarkable path winds upwards between terraced cornfields and mud-red farmhouses. Not much more than a shepherd's track, it climbs gently at first, past hens and snoozing dogs, then rises more steeply into a thickly wooded dell. Forty minutes later, through a clearing in the leaves, you get your first glimpse of stone. Then another – the crenelated crests of two watchtowers, peering over the tree line. Higher and higher the path climbs, tree roots becoming steps, branches becoming handholds. Then finally, hamstrings protesting, your destination looms into view: a sheer, inward-sloping wall of brick and white dolomite stone.

A stack of bricks has been fashioned into a precarious stairway; you're now inside a Ming Dynasty watchtower. The ash of an old campfire darkens the worn stone floor. Beside it, a second set of stone steps rises up to the top. Now you're back in open air, standing on the upper battlement of Zhengbei Tower, the highest point of the Jiankou section of Great Wall.

And all around you the world drops away. To the west, the crests of mountains plummet like a roller coaster, then rise again, the Great Wall flowing across the ridgeline into the hazy distance. To the south, far out of sight, is Beijing; from up here it might as well be centuries away.

Jiankou means 'arrow notch', named for the way the mountains hook around the flat-floored valley. It's also surely a reference to the weapon that proved so lethal in the hands of the warriors from beyond the Great Wall – the very reason for its existence in the first place. It's on quiet days, in places like Jiankou, when the romance of the wild Great Wall is conjured: miles of brick and stone, crumbling and overgrown, epic beyond imagination. A testament to the rise and fall of empires, of threats long vanished and military technologies long since superseded.

To journey west along the wall from here, you'd need climbing equipment and comprehensive insurance cover. Gravity-defying stretches with names like 'Soaring Eagle' and 'Sky Stair' beg the question: how did they build this, all those centuries ago? Hiking eastwards, the Great Wall tapers gently down mountains, and some hours later its wild battlements meet the upper reaches of the restored Mutianyu section. Climbing over a barricade onto smooth, recently laid cobbles, you're greeted by looks of astonishment from puffed-out tourists, who can only wonder at what discoveries lie beyond.

● **JIANKOU IS 1½** hours from Beijing. Take bus 916 from Dongzhimen to Huairou, then transfer to a taxi for the final stretch.

LES ARCHIVES DU CŒUR

At Christian Boltanski's installation *Les Archives du Cœur*, a 'heartbeat archive' in a plain building beside a scrubby Teshima Island cove, I entered the dark 'heart room'. Suddenly I was surrounded by the loud thump of a human heart, a single light pulsing in rhythm, glancing across black-mirrored walls. Recordings of heartbeats taken from thousands of people (and at least one Swedish dog) are played one after another, creating an oddly intimate experience – how often do you hear another person's heart, unless resting an ear on their chest? Stepping out of the dark, I went to the recording room and added my own beat to the library. –LAURA CRAWFORD

• TESHIMA IS ONE of the Seto Inland Sea islands that comprise Benesse Art Site, connected to the mainland by a ferry network.

KAIYNDY LAKE

Spears of spruce rise up from the water at this pristine lake, occupying an ear-popping location at 2000m (6600ft) of altitude, close to Kazakhstan's border with Kyrgyzstan. It owes its origins to the 1911 Kebin earthquake, which triggered a landslide in the Tian Shan mountains that submerged part of the forest here, and created a natural dam that trapped glacial waters and eventually brought the glassy, 400m/1312ft-wide Kaiyndy Lake into existence. Glowing an unearthly shade of turquoise and backed by forest-clad mountains, the sunken trees add to the mystique of this tranquil place and have made it a hit among divers.

• REACH KAIYNDY LAKE by car. On paved roads from Almaty it's about a 280km (174 mile) drive, east on the A351 then southwest.

CHIMI LHAKHANG

The raunchy teaching methods of a Buddhist sage are immortalised at this monastery in Punakha in Bhutan – where you might even be bonked on the head with a lucky phallus. The temple was built in honour of Lama Drukpa Kunley, who supposedly vanquished a demoness with a thunderbolt. A model of the righteous thunderbolt is here, along with prayer wheels and fertility shrines. Lama Drukpa Kunley, dubbed the 'Divine Madman', was a fan of thinking outside the box, so his teaching methods were allusive and rich in penis symbolism. Unsurprisingly, Chimi Lhakhang has become a favourite pilgrimage place for couples with fertility problems, who seek blessings, sometimes in the form of being struck on the head with a wooden member.

● **THE SHRINE IS** in Pangna village, accessed by a pathway from Sopsokha through ricefields before an uphill climb.

MAWSYNRAM & CHERRAPUNJEE, INDIA

MEGHALAYA TREE BRIDGES

Pinched between Bangladesh and Myanmar in India's far east, two regions are vying for the title of wettest place on Earth. Mawsynram and Cherrapunjee, both in Meghalaya state, harness this heroic rainfall into 'living bridges': walkways plaited together from rubber-tree roots. Weaving almost a kilometre of roots into a natural bridge takes skill. Hollow tree trunks are positioned strategically to guide their growth, and it can take more than a decade for the roots to strengthen in their unnatural new pose. The result is breathtaking: knotted root bridges blend into the lush Meghalaya forest, able to support the weight of up to 50 people. One of the longest bridges, at 50m (164ft), is 20km (12 miles) east of Cherrapunjee in Pynursla.

● **AT THE TIME** of writing, travel was not advised to the state of Meghalaya.

✳ OCEANIA

THIS PAGE: Glowworms scatter green light across New Zealand's Waitomo Caves (p113)

GLOUCESTER TREE

I always loved Enid Blyton's *The Magic Faraway Tree*, where adventures awaited at the top of an enchanted tree. But there's no whimsy about climbing up this fire-lookout tree – it's a distinctly precarious experience. Vicious-looking metal spikes driven into the tree trunk spiral upwards and it's a hand-over-hand climb, with only a flimsy bit of wire netting for reassurance. Having tried skydiving and abseiling, I reckon I'm up for a bit of exhilaration, but with nothing to stop me slipping between the spokes I freeze halfway up with sheer heart-hammering terror. So, sorry, I can't tell you if magical folk live at the top of the tree. Do let me know if you see them.

–TRACY WHITMEY

AFTER BEING CLIMBED for more than 50 years, the Gloucester Tree was cordoned off in 2023 but was slated to reopen with a 37m/121ft-high platform in 2026.

LAKE HILLIER

Look at any map and chances are that the bodies of water are coloured blue. But if you were to draw Middle Island, part of Australia's little-known Recherche Archipelago, you'd need a pink crayon (preferably of a bubblegum hue) to depict its most striking landmark: Lake Hillier. Unlike most coloured lakes, Hillier's hue is caused neither by reflection from the lakebed or the dye of seasonal bacteria: it's beta-carotene, produced by extremophile organisms that extract nutrients from the hypersaline water.

But unprecedented rainfall in 2022 decreased the lake's salinity, enabling green photosynthesising organisms to dominate over the extremophiles – except dealing a blow to Hillier's flamingo brilliance, which faded from sherbet to dusky rose. Receding water levels are the only remedy to restore its rosiness, but scientists have high hopes that Hillier will return to its former glory sometime soon.

MIDDLE ISLAND IS part of a wilderness area that's off-limits to tourists, but you can view Lake Hillier on a two-hour helicopter tour from Esperance.

THE DIVIDED CHURCH

The Bible reckons a house divided cannot stand, but the Ziona Church tells a different story; literally split in two, it's been a Ma'uke landmark since 1882.

The church was a joint project between two neighbouring villages of the same denomination; all was going a treat until the two fell out over the interior colour scheme. Arguments – pink versus red, teal against turquoise – enflamed the villages. Unable to reach a compromise, a wall was built across the middle of the church, separate entrances were constructed, and each village set to painting their side with a polychromatic passion. Though each flock finally had the rainbow rooms of their dreams, the decor dispute had taken its toll; while one congregation worshipped, the other would be right outside, playing noisy, disruptive games.

After years of cold-shoulder Sundays, a pastor finally convinced the villages to hold communal services. The wall came down, the church was given a neutral-palette makeover and villagers took turns singing hymns, though the separate entrances remained, and the pulpit – in the centre of the nave – retained a dividing line that speakers were (and still are) expected to straddle. This harmony holds today, so much so that the interior has been repainted in all of its original bold, clashing colours. Visitors are welcome to attend Sunday services (and to use whichever entrance they wish).

AIR RAROTONGA FLIES between Rarotonga and Ma'uke every day but Sunday.

KIRITIMATI

If you like to be in the right place at the right time, why not spend Christmas on Christmas Island? There's historical precedent: Captain Cook stopped here and named it on 24 December 1777. Kiritimati is pronounced 'Krismas' – 'ti' is pronounced 's' in the language of Kiribati, which, yes, is pronounced 'Kiribas'. Lying just above the equator in the Pacific Ocean, and remote from pretty much everywhere else, Kiritimati is the world's biggest coral atoll.

If you never thought you'd visit London, Paris, Poland and the wonderfully named Banana on the same day, think again; these are the practical, political or eccentrically personal names of the island's four early settlements. London is (of course) the capital of this former British colony. Paris (across the channel) and nearby Poland were named by a homesick Frenchman with aspirations to grandeur, and his Polish mechanic. The journey by boat across the channel is an adventure in itself, starting with finding a local boat owner willing to make the trip; there is no public water transport. And Banana? The site of the first banana gardens is still a sizeable village and minibuses heading to and from London offer a good opportunity to chat with locals.

After locating a car, and an owner willing to hire it out, take a road trip to visit the island's biggest population – seabirds. If you're used to looking up when bird-watching, here's a tip: on Kiritimati, look down. There are no Christmas trees (!), and the lack of tall vegetation means that birds such as boobies and terns breed on the ground. Towards the southeast end of the Bay of Wrecks – no prizes for guessing how that name came about – the road runs alongside a vast, noisy, smelly and completely fantastic breeding colony of sooty terns. In the salt-blasted shrubs, keep an eye open for *bokikokiko* (Kiritimati reed warblers); a big tick on the must-see list for serious birders.

East of the island's main lagoon, salt flats interspersed with shallow lagoons offer bountiful bonefish to fly-fishers. If it's too rough for a boat ride or you don't want to wade in the water, you can cast a line from the back of a pickup truck. Don't even think about doing this alone, though – it's extremely easy to get lost and sun-crazed in the island's interior, and going Christmas crackers is a sure way to ruin a marvellous adventure.

–*VIRGINIA JEALOUS*

FIJI AIRWAYS FLIES weekly to Kiritimati from Nadi (Fiji) and Honolulu (O'ahu, Hawai'i).

COCOS ISLANDS GOLF CLUB

It's an unusual location for a golf course, laid out as it is along an airport runway on a coral atoll in the middle of the Indian Ocean. I'm with a group of locals, pushing our carts along the tarmac. There's friendly banter when yet another ball disappears into the lagoon. Then the siren goes and we wait at the edge of the runway. Cold drinks emerge from golf bags. A heavy military aircraft approaches, lands, and taxis to the terminal; American soldiers from an oceanic base are stopping on their way to R & R in Australia. Their astonished faces peer through windows – as amused golfers, raising a glass to the new arrivals, peer back.

– VIRGINIA JEALOUS

COCOS' GOLF CLUB is on West Island. Flights to the islands depart from Perth.

FONUAFO'OU DISAPPEARING ISLAND

The British vessel HMS *Falcon* reported in 1865 that it had discovered a new landmass in the central part of the Tonga Islands, some 50m (164ft) high and 2km (1.2 miles) long. Naturally, they named it Falcon Island; unsurprisingly, that didn't last. Tonga immediately changed the name to Fonuafo'ou (or 'new land'), planted a flag and claimed it for the king. Not 30 years had passed before the island vanished in 1894, only to re-emerge from the Pacific two years later, even taller at 320m (1050ft). This ephemeral isle – the tip of an underwater volcano – has disappeared and reappeared at least five times over the years in a series of fiery eruptions. Current status: missing.

● **CHECK UP ON** Fonuafo'ou (presently a shoal) on the monthly ferry from Niuafo'ou to Vava'u.

FUTURO HOUSE

Visitors to the University of Canberra could be forgiven for thinking a UFO has landed on campus. Supported by four steel legs, the space-age, podlike structure may look like something from *The Jetsons* – complete with a hatch-like entry and drop-down staircase – but it's actually one of the world's few remaining examples of a Futuro House, designed by visionary Finnish architect Matti Suuronen in 1968. Originally intended as ski chalets or holiday houses, the prefabricated Futuros could be transported in several pieces and assembled in just a few days – or even airlifted in one piece by helicopter. The revolutionary design attracted global attention, but its fanfare was short-lived; the 1973 oil crisis pushed up the price of plastic (a key component of the buildings), customers cancelled their orders, and

only about 100 were ever constructed. Few were used as dwellings; some were turned into cafes or real-estate agencies in the USA, some were used as Swedish watchtowers, and this one was shifted around Canberra before eventually being used, fittingly, at an observatory. In 2011 the damaged and disused Futuro was donated to the university, where it was painstakingly restored and reassembled. Now it's a student workspace, and a must-see for anyone who has ever wondered what the future might look like.

* **FUTURO HOUSE IS** next to Building 5, at the University of Canberra; take bus 3 from City Bus Station.

AUSTRALIA'S BIG ROADSIDE ATTRACTIONS

Hilariously gigantic and wonderfully random, Australia's bizarre roadside attractions often have no business being where they are. Drive on and giggle at the outstanding oddity of each oversized art piece.

WOOMBYE, QUEENSLAND

1. BIG PINEAPPLE

Australia has a plethora of ridiculously oversized roadside attractions designed to attract passing traffic and distract kids from asking "are we there yet?" on long road trips. Sure, they're kitsch, but that's part of the fun. The Big Pineapple has been visited by the British royal family – and if it's good enough for royalty, it's good enough for you.

TAMWORTH, NEW SOUTH WALES

2. BIG GOLDEN GUITAR

Instrumental in cementing Tamworth's reputation as Australia's country-music capital, the Big Golden Guitar fronts a tourist centre that fittingly includes the National Guitar Museum.

5

8

Herald Sun Sunday
Souvenirs
Hot Donuts
NED KELLY

9

GIANT KOALA
Tourist complex
WELCOME
OPEN
GIANT
KOALA
complex

10

AUSTRALIA'S BIG ROADSIDE ATTRACTIONS

PENGUIN, TASMANIA

3. BIG PENGUIN

In a town called Penguin, where fairy-sized penguins come ashore, there was only one real contender for a signature statue: a 3m/10ft-high penguin with a beady glare, ceremoniously placed on the main road in 1975.

COFFS HARBOUR, NEW SOUTH WALES

4. BIG BANANA

As sunny as the smiles it elicits from passersby, the Big Banana adds visual ap-peel to its eponymous fun park, in which you can 'experience the world of bananas' at the on-site plantation.

KINGSTON, SOUTH AUSTRALIA

5. BIG LOBSTER

There are some cracks showing in this colossal crustacean, but that doesn't stop the locals loving him. 'Larry' has been enticing folk to a seafood restaurant since created by artist Paul Kelly in 1979. If only the kitchen had a supersized saucepan…

SARINA, QUEENSLAND

6. BIG CANE TOAD

After Hawaiian cane toads were imported to Australia to combat crop-guzzling beetles, the toad population swelled to hundreds of millions and continues to deplete native species. The town of Sarina ruminates on this self-inflicted disaster with a snarling toad named Buffy.

KIMBA, SOUTH AUSTRALIA

7. BIG GALAH

If you've ever seen this haughty bird in the wild, screeching and puffing its pink feathers, you'll understand the Aussie insult of calling someone a 'galah'. By contrast, the 8m/26ft-high galah statue on the Eyre Hwy looks almost regal.

GOULBURN, NEW SOUTH WALES

8. THE BIG MERINO

Ramming home the sentiment that Australia rode to prosperity on the sheep's back, this 15m/49ft-high, 18m/59ft-long 'Rambo' designed by architect Gary Dutallis, was built in 1985. It houses an exhibition on wool, with a viewing platform and shop.

GLENROWAN, VICTORIA

9. BIG NED KELLY

If you do the crime, you pay the time. However, if you're Australia's most infamous outlaw, you get immortalised by artist Kevin Thomas with a 6m/20ft-high fibreglass figure in the town where your gang had its last siege. Go figure.

DADSWELLS BRIDGE, VICTORIA

10. GIANT KOALA

On the Western Hwy at the edge of the Grampians (Gariwerd) National Park, this towering critter made by artist Ben van Zetten was renamed Sam in memory of a koala that suffered burns in a bushfire and later died of chlamydia.

CAPE LEEUWIN

This rugged headland, overseen by its 1895 lighthouse, is the most southwesterly point on the Australian mainland. To its south lie the wild waters of the Southern Ocean; next landfall is Antarctica. To its west the equally wild – if less frigid – waters of the Indian Ocean link Australia with Africa. The Cape is the spot where these two mighty oceans meet.

If the vagaries of light, weather, tide and swell allow, it's possible for a lucky visitor to see this merging of the waters. A distinct line becomes visible offshore, marking the point where the two oceans reach this end of their journeys. Standing near the cliff edge at the edge of the continent, it's an elemental experience.

● **THE CLOSEST TOWNSHIP,** Augusta, is 320km (199 miles) by road from Perth.

GNOMESVILLE

It may be little more than a humble roundabout, but for some 6000 painted pixies, Gnomesville is the capital of the great Gnoman Empire – its citizens posed in planes, in trains and partaking in every imaginable pastoral pastime. A local is said to have placed a solitary garden gnome in the hollow of a tree here in the 1990s. Fearing it was lonely, other townspeople followed suit. The population has grown exponentially ever since, as visitors from around the world flock to Western Australia to drop off their beloved gnomes. Locals say Gnomesville's success as a tourist attraction has been so phe-gnome-nal that the population is slowly creeping onto private land. Gnomes placed outside the city limits are allegedly retrieved and brought to Gnomesville proper, where they are placed in a designated 'gnome jail'.

● **GNOMESVILLE IS IN** Ferguson Valley, 35km (22 miles) inland from Bunbury by car.

WAITOMO GLOWWORM CAVES

New Zealand isn't short on otherworldly oddities; after all, this is a country that's made a fortune marketing itself as the ideal backdrop for big-budget fantasy films. But of all its curious attractions, the North Island's Waitomo Glowworm Caves may just be the most surreal. Visitors descend from the enchanted forests above into an underground cave discovered 120 years ago by local Māori chief Tane Tinorau. They then hop aboard a boat and float down the underground Waitomo River into a glow-in-the-dark wonderland known as Glowworm Grotto, where thousands of tiny critters are hard at work emitting a turquoise glow. It's here that the roof of the cave morphs into a psychedelic planetarium with untold galaxies of living lights.

Despite their name, Waitomo's resident population of *Arachnocampa luminosa* aren't actually worms;

they're fungus gnats. Endemic to New Zealand, they thrive in its damp caves and become luminescent in both the larval and imago stages (the latter is the last stage an insect attains during metamorphosis). Though found throughout the country, nowhere is there a colony quite as large or flamboyant as in caves of Waitomo. Even if you hate damp and dark spaces, or are the kind of person who absolutely detests bugs, it's hard not to be enchanted by the spectacular subterranean kingdom of these bioluminescent maggots.

OPEN DAILY, 9AM to 5pm. Many hop-on hop-off buses from Auckland include the caves in their passes.

COOBER PEDY'S GRASSLESS GOLF COURSE

Mining towns tend to be pretty soulless places inhabited by gruff grunts and slick-suited businesspeople with dollar signs for eyeballs. I don't visit these places. But then I heard about a mining town located in the rear end of the Australian outback that was anything but typical. Flying into Coober Pedy, though, I couldn't spot a town anywhere in sight. In fact, it looked like a team of extremely large, hungry earthworms had invaded the land below, leaving behind towering pits of rubble and little else. Turns out those holes are mines, and what you find in them are opals. Lots of opals. In fact, an estimated 80% of the world's supply comes from Coober Pedy.

Vibrant, too, is the life residents have carved out of this burnt-red earth. Yanni Athanasiadis, who developed the Umoona Opal Mine, has travelled the world but keeps coming back to Coober Pedy. "When I first came here from Greece years ago, I said, 'Oh no. What have I done?'" he recalled, as we toured his underground home. However, after sleeping beneath the earth for decades, he tells me he couldn't imagine ever living above ground again. Dugouts like this one maintain a pleasant year-round temperature of about 24°C (75°F), making them a great escape from outback extremes. Coober Pedy also features glorious subterranean churches and cavernous underground hotels. Yet its most curious attraction may be the one above ground.

There's only one golf club in the world with reciprocal rights at the 'home of golf', St Andrews – and it's right here in Coober Pedy. The daytime heat is so oppressive that I opt to play at night with a glow-in-the-dark golf ball. The only grass this ball will touch is the carpet of artificial turf I'm holding in my hand for teeing. The rest of the 18-hole course is utterly lunar-like in appearance. It's also so difficult that the last of my three glowing balls goes missing down one of Coober Pedy's signature wormholes, destined to become yet another shimmering orb lost to its kaleidoscopic underworld.

—MARK JOHANSON

FIVE FLIGHTS PER week link Coober Pedy with Adelaide. Pay your green fees at Opalios on Hutchison St.

NORTHERN TERRITORY, AUSTRALIA

HENLEY ON TODD REGATTA

A uniquely Australian boat race that takes place on a dry riverbed (yes, dry), the Henley on Todd Regatta was first held in 1962 to poke fun at the formality of traditional British regattas (ie, those held in water). 'Boats' made from metal frames covered in advertising are carried, pushed or pulled by 'rowers', culminating in the Battle of the Gunboats – trucks modified to resemble boats, armed with confetti bombs and water hoses (warning: despite this being a dry race, spectators may still get wet). The spectacle is whimsical, nonsensical and a whole lot of fun – there's lots of opportunities to participate, including a BYO boat category.

● **THE RACE IS** annually on the third Saturday in August, on the Todd River outside Alice Springs.

LAND DIVERS OF PENTECOST ISLAND

If you thought bungee jumping was madness, wait till you meet the people who invented it. They start building the wooden towers in April. Young men work feverishly in the jungle, sawing and tying, measuring platform heights and sturdiness. When they're ready, village teenagers will fling themselves off headfirst, with only a liana vine tied around each ankle to break the fall. All this in the hope of a successful yam harvest!

This is Pentecost Island's ancient *naghol* (land diving). A test of courage and rite of passage, it's heart-stopping to watch, like a terrible accident unfolding – but soon enough come cheers and singing, as the young diver pulls up with a snap, his head barely grazing the ground.

● **NAGHOL TAKES PLACE** weekly from April to June. There are twice-weekly flights from Port Vila to Lonorore on Pentecost Island; day trips can be organised from Port Vila.

GIBBS FARM

It's a sculpture gallery, it's a science show, it's home to Tibetan yak and water buffalo: Gibbs Farm is a genre-straddling open-air experience. Located on the Kaipara Harbour, along the northwestern coast of New Zealand's North Island, it was commissioned by millionaire businessperson and art patron Alan Gibbs, and has 29 huge artworks displayed against a sweeping backdrop of rolling greenery, coastal waters and shimmering mudflats. As the Southern Hemisphere's largest harbour, this is an epic canvas for contemporary artists; some, like Anish Kapoor and Marijke de Goey, created their largest works here. The scale is truly thrilling. Richard Serra's *Te Tuhirangi Contour* sweeps across the hills, bracketing the land like a gigantic steel punctuation mark. Moulded on a natural rock formation, *Zhan Wang's Floating Island of Immortals* shimmers in a pool of water, equal parts organic and futuristic. And although it isn't included in tours of the site, *Electrum*, by Eric Orr and Greg Leyh, is a work of mind-blowing imagination. Looking a bit like a four-storey-high lollipop, and topped by a spherical Faraday cage to protect its operator, it features the world's largest Tesla coil, harnessing over three million volts and flinging them out in retina-blasting bolts. The massive voltage sucks electrons from the surrounding air, letting rip 15m/49ft-long streams of electricity in crackling arcs – instant lightning.

● **GIBBS FARM IS** open to the public for self-guided tours only by prearrangement on specified days. Book free tickets in advance online.

TO THE ENDS OF THE EARTH

NEW ZEALAND (AOTEAROA)

SOUTH ISLAND (TE WAIPOUNAMU)

Sparsely populated and buffeted by westerly winds, New Zealand's South Island (Te Waipounamu) is much wilder than its neighbour to the north. The Southern Alps run down the South Island like a spine, and the West Coast is a mood board of nature's ferocity: wave-smashed cliffs, rivers powered by glacial melt, and rainforests threaded by tannin-stained streams.

Glorious wilderness isn't the only drawcard. The South Island is also brimming with novel sights, like Whataroa's one-of-a-kind heron breeding site, and an ends-of-the-Earth landmark with gale-flattened trees. Many visitors come purely for solitude, to seek respite on odyssey-length hikes or cruise into the 'Place of Silence' – but living here full-time demands resilience. Spend time on the South Island and you'll soon soak up the locals' dry humour and can-do spirit.

● **RENT A CAR** to visit the South Island's obscure corners. Start in Dunedin (3½ hours from Queenstown's international airport) and drive clockwise around the coast, allowing plenty of time for winding roads. Book cruises from Manapouri in advance.

TO THE ENDS OF THE EARTH

TUNNEL BEACH, *NEAR DUNEDIN*

The South Island is rich in soul-stirring coves, but one in particular feels like a portal to an unearthly realm: Tunnel Beach. Its passageway was carved into the sandstone in the 1870s, and spiny remnants of fossilised sea creatures are still visible in the rock. As you emerge on the other side, you face the angry ocean from a beach of dove-grey sand. Let the roaring waves quiet your mind.

SLOPE POINT, *NEAR CURIO BAY*

Land's end on the South Island is a bright yellow sign declaring the distances to the equator and South Pole (5140km/3194 miles and 4803km/2985 miles respectively). It's only a short walk from the trailhead, but Antarctic winds are against you the entire way – expect your hood to inflate like a parachute. Note the thatch of trees by the trail, so blasted by the unobstructed wind that they grip the earth at a 45-degree angle.

DOUBTFUL SOUND, *FIORDLAND*

The epic fjords and peaks of Milford Sound draw more than a million annual visitors, leaving nearby Doubtful Sound to live up to its Māori name: Patea, the 'Place of Silence'. Cruise boats ply the midnight-dark waters, and there are no human settlements for hundreds of miles in any direction – just the hiss of waterfalls and the occasional splash of fur seals flopping into the fjord.

KŌTUKU BREEDING GROUND, *WHATAROA*

Māori traditions say it's lucky to see a kōtuku (white heron); in Whataroa, then, you'll be showered by good fortune. This is the world's only known nesting site for these rare, lace-winged birds. White Heron Sanctuary Tours takes you into the reserve to watch these pearl-white birds swoop down from 1000-year-old trees to preen like dancers in the marsh.

PANCAKE ROCKS, *PUNAKAIKI*

Even the rocks seem alive at Paparoa National Park, where icy waves foam up through blowholes, and limestone crags look like human silhouettes. The most intriguing landform is at Punakaiki, where 30 million years of geological pressure have created spindles of limestone that look curiously like stacks of pancakes, thanks to imperfections in the rock.

THIS PAGE: Cattle plod beneath wind-flattened trees at Slope Point **PREVIOUS PAGE:** Punakaiki's limestone towers stretch to the misty horizon

HOKITIKA WILDFOODS FESTIVAL

I'm trying not to gag, but there's a cockroach in my mouth. It's artfully presented in a dainty cup of pink jelly, but there's no hiding that it's a massive bug. At least it's not still alive, unlike the grasshoppers at the next stall. The roach kept down – just – what next? Earthworm sushi, pickled huhu grubs, giant chocolate-coated beetles, mountain oysters (sheeps' testicles) – the Hokitika Wildfoods Festival is not for the fainthearted or the weak-stomached. I can't bring myself to swallow a huhu grub. As it is, for the rest of the day I'm picking cockroach feelers from between my teeth. *–TRACY WHITMEY*

THE FESTIVAL IS held annually on the second Saturday in March in Hokitika, on New Zealand's South Island.

SS AYRFIELD

Plenty of cities sink decommissioned cargo ships to create artificial reefs, but what happens when you let a 1140-tonne (1257-ton) hunk of steel languish on the water for over 50 years? In the case of the SS *Ayrfield*, you get a majestic 'floating forest' where mangroves fight for space atop a rusted hull. Built in 1911, the *Ayrfield* helped the Australian government deliver supplies to US troops in the Pacific during WWII (when it was known as SS *Corrimal*), then ran supplies between Sydney and Newcastle until 1972, when it was sent to a breaking yard in Homebush Bay. It remains there alongside three other decommissioned ships, but none feature such spectacular foliage. The oft-photographed *Ayrfield's* resident mangroves have flourished, billowing over both sides of the hull and slowly ripping the ship apart; it may have survived a war and evaded dismemberment, but it's only a matter of time before it succumbs to nature.

TAKE THE TRAIN from Sydney's Central Station to Rhodes. Cross Bennelong Bridge for the best views.

RED-CRAB MIGRATION

If you're on Christmas Island at the start of the rainy season, be sure to drive very, very carefully. It's the time of the annual red-crab migration, and these little fellas have just one thing in mind. Cars, trucks, bicycles – all become insignificant, compared to the overwhelming urge to procreate.

Triggered by the first droplets of rain, crabs crawl from underground burrows deep in the forest and start their slow sideways creep to the beaches, some 8km (5 miles) away. Within hours the trickle becomes a rolling red tide of tens of millions of grumpy-faced crabs, driven on by their deep-rooted impulse to mate, and hellbent on making it to the sea. It's an instinctive but tight schedule: migration, burrow digging, wooing and mating must all be timed to coincide with a receding high-tide during the moon's last quarter. Only then will females shimmy into the surf to spawn precious eggs.

So, it's no wonder that nothing stands in their way. Scaling cliff faces, clinging to jagged rocks, fighting swarms of yellow crazy ants, the crabs lurch inexorably onwards. Despite road closures, crab fences and purpose-built underpasses, hordes of crabs play chicken with local traffic – rangers armed with plastic rakes patrol the streets, scooping them out of harm's way. Drivers should be thankful for this: the crabs' shells are tough enough to cause punctures.

● **CHRISTMAS ISLAND CAN** be reached by air from Perth (Australia) and Jakarta (Indonesia).

THE HEART OF VOH

In normal circumstances, the words 'romantic' and 'mangrove swamp' rarely occur in the same sentence, but in the north of New Caledonia's main island of Grande Terre, the local mangroves seem to have learnt about romance. In an extraordinary show of passion, they have grown to form a natural heart shape that has local microlight pilots in a spin. Best observed from above, La Cœur de Voh has spawned a new business, with enthusiastic romantics taking to the skies to see it – adding a whole new meaning to 'love is in the air'. Catch it while you can – rising sea levels caused by climate change have seen the heart fade in recent years.

AT THE TIME of writing, travel was not advised to New Caledonia.

UNDERWATER POST OFFICE

Here's a little something to add to any list you may have of things you never dreamed of doing, but totally need to accomplish now that you know they're possible. Things like, say, sending mail underwater. In a marine sanctuary just off the shores of Vanuatu's Hideaway Island there lies an underwater post office where visitors can dive 3m (10ft) down and drop off mail. This official branch of the Vanuatu Post accepts waterproof postcards that are embossed with an inkless stamp by scuba-diving postal workers. While their brethren on land fight off neighbourhood attack dogs, the intrepid postal workers of Hideaway Island need only to fend away a few curious reef sharks.

OPENING HOURS ARE posted on the beach at Hideaway Island resort. A floating flag denotes the post office location.

RUNIT DOME

On a tranquil coral atoll surrounded by turquoise water lies something that looks like a half-buried UFO – but the reality is much more sinister. In 1958, a US nuclear detonation (dubbed the 'Cactus test') left a huge crater on Runit Island. Other nuclear tests in the surrounding area led to high levels of contamination, and something had to be done to clean it up. So, in the late 1970s, the radioactive debris was mixed with contaminated topsoil, dumped in the crater, and sealed beneath a 46cm/18in-thick concrete dome. As the concrete decays, Marshall Islanders have been urging the US government to help with a clean-up, before the dome lives up to its ominous nickname: 'The Tomb'.

● **RUNIT CAN BE** seen by boat from neighbouring islands – since it's home to radioactive waste, visiting is not recommended.

WAITAVALA WATERSLIDE

Steamy, dreamy Taveuni seems purpose-built for doing sweet nothing. But too many days of languid lolling was making me feel as if I'd been bonked on the head by a coconut. It was time for action, and on Fiji's Garden Island, 'action' means only one thing: waterslide! No chlorinated chute here; this is a slick, scenic series of smooth-rock cascades that slice through the rainforest with surprising speed.

Wobbling on slippery boulders, I gawked as the local kids surfed, goofed and grandstanded down the gushing slide. Me? I went down on my bum, hit every bump and plonked into the water below with all the grace of a drunk giraffe. But injuries, indignity and all: it was the ride of a lifetime. *–TAMARA SHEWARD*

● **THE SLIDE, ON** the Waitavala Estate, is a 20-minute walk from Waiyevo on Taveuni's west coast.

TAUMATAWHA
GIHANGAKO
AUOTAMATEAT
KAKAPIKIMAU
HORONUKU
WHENUAKITAN

AKATANAUTURIPUNGAPOKAINATAHU

Were it not for its monstrous moniker, few people would bother to visit this unassuming hill. But, with 85 letters, it's the longest single-word place name in the world, according to the Guinness World Records. Roughly translated, it means 'the summit where Tamatea, the man with the big knees, the slider, climber of mountains, the land-swallower who travelled about, and played his nose flute to his lost loved one'. What a name! According to the legend, Māori explorer Tamatea fought a battle near the hill during which his beloved brother was killed. Grieving, Tamatea lingered near the battle site, playing a lament to his lost brother on a *kōauau,* or Māori flute. Locals just call it Taumata Hill.

TAUMATA HILL IS near Pōrangahau in Hawke's Bay on New Zealand's North Island (Te Ika-a-Māui). A sign displaying the name is situated 5km (3 miles) along Wimbledon Rd.

TREMENDOUS TREES

These towering and peaceful giants of the natural world have long been revered for their beauty, utility and strength. Discover the best areas around the world to encounter the most marvellous of these wise, wooded beings.

NEW SOUTH WALES, AUSTRALIA

1. WOLLEMI PINE

Believed to have died out with the dinosaurs, the Wollemi pine experienced a second coming when it was rediscovered in 1994. The cliffs and canyons of Wollemi National Park guard these rare conifers; you can also meet one in Sydney's Botanic Gardens.

NORTH ISLAND (TE IKA-A-MĀUI), NEW ZEALAND (AOTEAROA)

2. PŌHUTUKAWA

These fiery myrtle trees drape New Zealand's coasts with crimson in November and December. Māori mythology upholds that Cape Reinga's sacred pōhutukawa is the departure point for souls of the dead.

4

6

9

10

TREMENDOUS TREES

SOUTH ASIA
3. INDIAN BANYAN

Though their dangling fronds evoke Rapunzel's tresses, banyans are more parasite than fairy-tale maiden; they take root in other trees and slowly throttle them. The largest living example is the Great Banyan, draped over some 1.4 hectares (3.5 acres) of Acharya Jagadish Chandra Bose Indian Botanic Gardens near Kolkata.

CALIFORNIA, USA
4. GIANT SEQUOIA

Wider than two pickup trucks and scarred by endless wildfires, giant sequoias are true survivors. The biggest and burliest is the General Sherman Tree, an emblem of Sequoia National Park at almost 84m (276ft) tall.

CHILE & SOUTHERN ARGENTINA
5. ALERCE

South America's biggest and oldest tree species can grow for as long as 4000 years, slowly expanding its trunk to a diameter of 9m (30ft). The Gran Abuelo alerce in Chile's Parque Nacional Alerce Costero may be even older, at some 5400 years.

CENTRAL & EASTERN CHINA
6. YULAN MAGNOLIA

The sweet fragrance of magnolia first wafted from these hardy trees 95 million years ago. Today their blushing blooms garnish festivals and palaces around China – and gardens around the world.

BAJA CALIFORNIA, MEXICO
7. BOOJUM TREE

More alien than tree, the boojum resembles a spiky tentacle writhing its way out of the desert soil. As one of the world's slowest-growing trees, it stretches only 2cm to 5cm (0.8in to 2in) each year.

YEMEN
8. DRAGON'S BLOOD TREE

Calligraphic branches radiate out from the trunk of this Socotra Archipelago native. Its sticky, ruby-coloured resin is heralded as a cure-all, owing to its mystical origins in a battle between dragon and elephant (guess who won).

NAMIBIA & SOUTH AFRICA
9. QUIVER TREE

This aloe tree has defensive leaves forming a punk-rock crown above its pale trunk. As the name suggests, it resembles a clutch of feathered arrows, waiting to be pulled out and fired. In fact, bygone peoples hollowed out its branches for this very use... form *and* function!

SIEM REAP, CAMBODIA
10. STRANGLER FIG

When parasitic trees choose human structures as their host, the results are poetic. At Siem Reap, strangler figs have collided with ancient temple ruins, almost as though nature's hand is bringing humankind's constructed creations gently back down to Earth.

HOT WATER BEACH

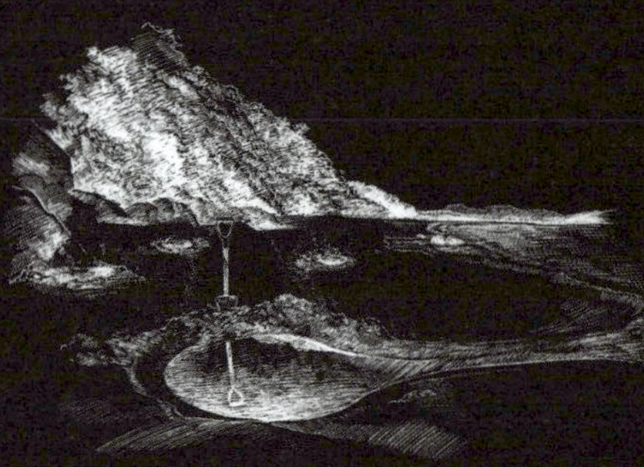

A rumour reached my ears about a mythical spot on New Zealand's North Island, where a steamy geothermal spring fizzles to the surface from golden sands. The rumour-monger spoke of a small window either side of low tide when the beach becomes a DIY spa. I arrived in the Coromandel Peninsula and strolled along Mercury Bay until I found a group of beachgoers bent over like gophers digging up heated holes. I joined the burrowing brigade and fashioned myself a sandy tub, but when I jumped in I instantly burnt my bum pink in the mineral-rich waters. It seems the rumour-monger forgot one important tip: use the ocean to control the temperature. –*MARK JOHANSON*

BUS IT FROM Auckland to Whitianga, then catch the seasonal bus to Hot Water Beach.

GIANT PINK SLUGS OF MT KAPUTAR

Arrive at Mt Kaputar National Park on a stormy night and you're in for a slimy surprise: a creature as wet as your tongue, as long as a cucumber and as fluorescent-pink as a nylon tutu. Picture, if you dare, a giant hot-pink slug. These startling slitherers (*Triboniophorus aff. graeffei*) are found only on remote Mt Kaputar in Australia's Nandewar Range, and spend most of their time feeding underground – but after rain, they rise to the surface to dine on lichen and tree moss. Remarkably, they're but one of many endemic invertebrates who've lived here in relative isolation for millions of years – from geometrically decorated red triangle slugs to cannibal land snails. Scientists say this unique habitat offers a unique glimpse into Australia's geological past.

● **MT KAPUTAR NATIONAL** Park is a 30km (19 mile) drive east of Narrabri, with campgrounds and bushwalking areas.

UMPHERSTON SINKHOLE (BALUMBUL)

For an erstwhile sheep station, the South Australian city of Mount Gambier is rich in natural wonders: there's the namesake volcano, the oat-milk-coloured cliffs of the Limestone Coast, and the Blue Lake (Warwar), which glows electric blue between November and March – thanks to the alchemy of warm temperatures and microscopic salt crystals. But the Umpherston Sinkhole, on the east side of the city, stands out as an unexpected fusion of natural beauty and artistic vision.

The sinkhole appeared when a cave roof collapsed and exposed a 50m/164ft-wide pit. Sudden sinkholes aren't unheard of around Mount Gambier, where the action of rain on limestone bedrock has gradually eked out a honeycomb of subterranean caves. Scottish settler James Umpherston saw potential in the city's eyesore in 1886, and set about transforming the pit into a garden.

After his death, it was abandoned and relegated to the ignoble fate of a rubbish dump.

By the 1970s, locals were restless to re-beautify Mount Gambier and they restored the sinkhole to a glorious garden: spindly palm trees fringe the edges, cloudlike hydrangeas spill from flower beds, and ivy wreaths the steep walls. Visitors can follow a circular walkway that spirals down into the sinkhole. By night, it's illuminated by dozens of sparkling eyes, as possums scamper along the limestone shelves – the lucky inhabitants of this low-lying Eden.

THE SINKHOLE IS 3km (2 miles) east of Mount Gambier's Central Business District, and it's free to visit. Take your time descending; each terrace affords a different view of its craggy limestone shelves and flourishing greenery.

GARAAN-NGADDIM (HORIZONTAL WATERFALLS)

On the north coast of Australia's Kimberley region, the movement of the tides creates a 'horizontal waterfall' through a 300m/984ft-wide gorge. Known as Garaan-ngaddim, this place has held profound significance for the Dambeemangaddee people, the native title holders of land and sea here, for more than 56,000 years.

"Our ancestors have given us this Country to look after," explains Leah Umbagai, Vice Chair of Dambimangari Aboriginal Corporation. "We want visitors to feel welcome and safe, to see, feel and respect Country the way we do."

Garaan-ngaddim ('floating over') was carved out by the Woongudd woman (spiritual snake) who struck the land with her writhing tail as she moved. Woongudd's creative powers are active whenever the waters move, and when the tide ebbs she is at rest.

"Our old people, the Woddorda people, would travel between the islands, using the tides to travel," says Umbagai. "Our old people would only travel through the gaps for a specific purpose and always at the right time: neap tides, smooth waters, to show respect for Woongudd."

Garaan-ngaddim is a place for quiet reflection. By visiting respectfully, visitors can listen to what Country reveals to them. "When we look after Country the right way, Wandjina [creator spirits] look after us," explains Umbagai. 'Country is happy, people are happy."

THE DAMBIMANGARI ABORIGINAL Corporation is working with the tourism industry on sensitive ways for visitors to experience Garaan-ngaddim. Look for cultural tour guides at the falls – the best way to ensure an enriching and sensitive visit – and see inspiration and cultural background on its website (dambimangari.com.au).

LAKE BALLARD

Lake Ballard is a salt lake, hazy as a mirage under outback sun. In this isolated landscape it's hard to tell if I'm looking at land or sky, or to imagine who or what made the tracks that meander between solitary figures dotted across the lake's surface. These 51 metal statues collectively form *Inside Australia*, British sculptor Antony Gormley's representation of the 51 residents of nearby township Menzies. Walking onto the lake, distance is deceptive. It's as if the figures are swimming in and out of focus, in and out of reach. Later I return at full moon, adding another perspective to this extraordinary place.

–VIRGINIA JEALOUS

LAKE BALLARD IS 51km (32 miles) from Menzies by road, and 200km (124 miles) from the nearest airport at Kalgoorlie.

WORLD'S STEEPEST STREET

Fans of optical illusions take note: there's a 350m/1148ft-long residential street in Aotearoa's South Island city of Dunedin where, if you snap a photo at an angle, all the houses appear to be sinking into the ground. Historians say the steepness of Baldwin St – which has a gradient of about 35% – was unintentional and merely the result of a city grid built with little regard for local topography. Nowadays it's a local badge of honour; so much so, that Baldwin St is in a years-long tug-of-war with rival road Ffordd Pen Llech in Wales for the coveted 'world's steepest street' title from Guinness World Records. Regardless of who's on top in a given year, Baldwin St has its fun by hosting an annual race known as the Gutbuster – see if you can beat the locals sprinting uphill (the current record is one minute, 56 seconds).

OPEN TO TRAFFIC year-round, Baldwin St is about 3.5km (2.2 miles) northeast of Dunedin's city centre.

VICTORIA, AUSTRALIA

ARADALE ASYLUM

Preventing inpatients from escaping can still be aesthetically pleasing, according to the architects of Aradale Asylum. Modelled after the barracks-style asylums fashionable in 19th-century England, this 70-building complex was established for the care of people with mental illnesses in the then-colony of Victoria. Italianate features like campanile towers and archways bestowed a certain elegance, and connecting bridges and arcades were unique design features for an asylum. By building sunken fences around the compound, architects GW Vivian and John James Clark ensured iron-clad security while preserving countryside views (and maintaining the illusion of freedom for unhappy patients).

This psychiatric hospital held hundreds of people, both patients and prisoners, over 126 years before closing in 1993. Though guided tours of the asylum whisper of ghostly sightings, it's the history of patients' isolation, and their ability to endure unproven psychiatric 'care', that will haunt you long after your visit – note the frantic scratch marks on the inside of wooden doors.

● **ROAM THESE ECHOING** halls by guided tour. Audience participation (knocking on doors, lying on a mortician's slab...) is unfortunately mandatory. It's 2½ hours by road from Melbourne.

YAP, MICRONESIA

RAI STONES

What is money? Chances are you pay for things with fancy paper or a plastic card, but the people of Yap, in Micronesia, use giant limestone wheels for ceremonial transactions. Though perhaps no crazier than waving a flimsy piece of plastic over a card reader, the choice of stone is unusual, given there isn't a single source of limestone on the island. So where did Yap get all of its so-called rai stones? Local lore has it that 500 years ago some fisherfolk washed up in Palau, 400km (249 miles) away, and traded goods for quarried limestone. The stones were then carved, brought back to Yap by canoe, and refashioned into donut-shaped discs that served as the island's main currency. As rai stones can measure up to 3m (10ft) high and weigh 5 tonnes (5.5 tons), they're rarely moved; ownership is simply recorded in the oral history.

● **UNITED AIRLINES OFFERS** a few flights each week to Yap via Guam or Palau.

EUROPE

THIS PAGE: A stone bell tower breaks the surface of turquoise Reschensee, Italy (p155)

SINTRA, PORTUGAL

QUINTA DA REGALEIRA WELLS

The spiral staircases of these towers aren't just forbidding: they represent a journey from death to rebirth. Hints at dark alchemy are scattered around the UNESCO-protected estate of Quinta da Regaleira – a flamboyant blend of Gothic, Moorish and Renaissance architectural styles – especially around its showy gardens. Beneath this lavish residence, commissioned by coffee tycoon António Carvalho Monteiro in 1904, burrow two wells. But there's no water: these hidden tunnels were once used in secretive Masonic initiation rites. One has nine moss-rimmed levels, hinting at Dante's nine circles of Hell and Heaven, across its 27m (89ft) height. The other has straight staircases, with steps numbered according to Masonic principles, descending to a huge Knights Templar cross.

● **QUINTA DA REGALEIRA** is open daily; it's located 700m (2297ft) west of central Sintra.

FALKIRK, SCOTLAND

THE KELPIES

The giant horses of Scotland's Forth & Clyde Canal toss their heads in a display of equine strength – or rather, the strength of Scotland's waterways.

In Scottish folklore, kelpies are water-dwelling spirits in the shape of horses, who carry humans on their backs before drowning them. Occasionally they take the form of comely young men or women, who lure virgins into the spirit world. Fortunately, this glittering steel sculpture has no such malign intent. Towering 30m (98ft) above the Helix parklands, the *Kelpies* overlook the eastern entrance to the Forth & Clyde Canal, built as a key transport route across central Scotland. Clydesdale horses once tugged barges along Scotland's canals, and artist Andy Scott considered them an apt symbol of the might of the country's waterways and its industrial heritage.

● **YOU CAN GLIMPSE** the sculptures from the M9 between Falkirk and Grangemouth, or take a guided tour and step inside.

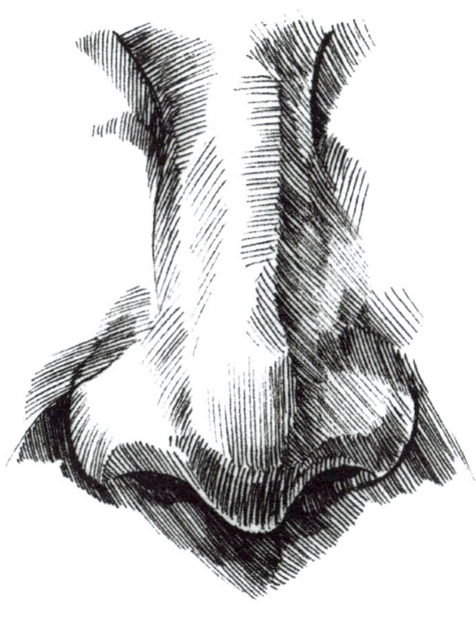

LUND NASOTEKET

It's not easy getting your hooter immortalised in a *nasothek* – a collection of noses. These carefully curated repositories are an exclusive affair, solely open to just the finest of human facial protuberances. Only the most distinguished of nostrils need apply. And the *nasothek* at Sweden's Lund University is the most extensive collection of its kind in Europe; since 1986 it has assembled more than 100 casts of human schnozzes. Each one is decided through a guarded process of nomination and debate. Authors, doctors and local legends have offered their noses to immortality, enduring a very public plaster-cast process. It's hoped that this illustrious collection of conks will inspire younger members of the university.

● **THIS COLLECTION ON** Sandgatan 2 in Lund is open weekdays (term time), 9am to 6pm.

ICELANDIC PHALLOLOGICAL MUSEUM

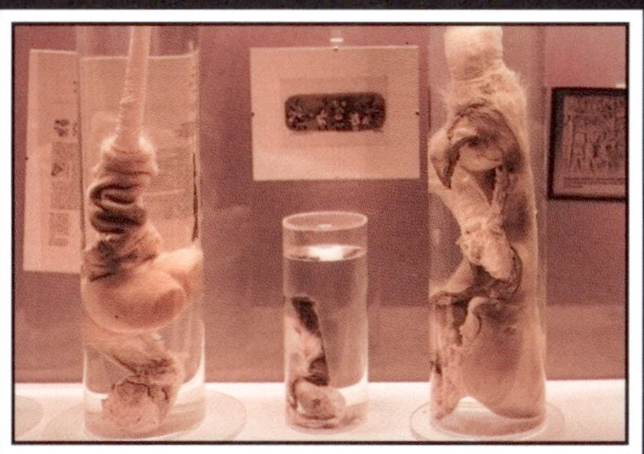

"Stop your juvenile giggling, they'll deny you entry." My then boyfriend, an Australian fond of innuendo, was directing a photoshoot: me with a casual arm around a gigantic sculpture of a penis in Húsavik, on Iceland's remote north coast. But neither of us could suppress tears of laughter as we entered the Phallological Museum and viewed the world's largest collection of penises, the phallic tribute to the Iceland Olympic handball team, and the 'waiting list' of human donors. The museum moved in 2011, and again in 2020; it's now blatantly out and proud (sorry) in Reykjavík, with a penis-themed bistro and its first human donation: the pickled pecker of a 95-year-old Icelander. *–KARYN NOBLE*

● **THE MUSEUM IS** in the heart of Reykjavík at Reykjastræti 4, Hafnartorg, and opens 10am to 7pm daily.

PAMUKKALE-HIERAPOLIS

High above the village of Pamukkale (meaning Cotton Castle) lie the famous travertines: limpid pools of turquoise water set in chalk-white trays of calcium carbonate shaped like giant waterlily leaves. Sans shoes, visitors tiptoe up through the pools to the plateau above. There, in the Pamukkale Termal, better-heeled swimmers can take to waters that are the temperature of a soothing bath. Beneath them, the snapped-off trunks of ancient columns offer evocative testimony to the existence of a spa here since Greco-Roman times.

So stunning are the travertines that they tend to overshadow the ruins of ancient Hierapolis, straddling the hillside above them. Yet the ruins here can give even better-known Ephesus a run for its money. The huge theatre shows off the wealth and importance of the old city that once stood on the plateau – from its tiered stone seats, visitors can all but see the actors of antiquity striding on to the stage. Nearby, the apostle Saint Philip was crucified upside down, a dastardly deed commemorated by an octagonal martyrium to which pilgrims used to flock. Flagstones still line Frontinus St, where visitors can follow the ancients as far as a toilet block designed to accommodate multiple bottoms. A ruinous gate opens on to a necropolis of house-sized tombs that sprawls for 2km (1.2 miles), silent but for the hoots of the owls.

● **VISITORS CAN STAY** the night in Pamukkale village and walk up to the travertines via one of three trails. Make sure to review current travel advisories before planning a trip.

MACOCHA ABYSS

Your stomach tightens as you look down into the gorge. There are 138m (453ft) of steep, lichen-splattered walls, dropping to a mossy floor that seems to beckon malevolently.

The feeling of nervous awe when you stand at a great height – and the irrational fear that you might step into the abyss – is known as *l'appel du vide* (the call of the void). To neuroscientists, these intrusive thoughts are common when our anxious brains perceive a steep drop. Our self-preservation instincts make us vividly imagine the fate we hope to avoid.

Places like the Macocha Abyss, with its sheer limestone walls and shadowy depths, inspire these unsettling inklings – and often come with dark folklore attached. According to one Czech tale, a woman lured her stepson to the gorge and threw him in (macocha means stepmother). She later leapt in after him following the death of her own biological son – though in other tellings, the stepmother was thrown in by furious members of her community. Either way, the abyss had to be fed.

This gorge, formed by a collapsed cave, is 30km (19 miles) northeast of Brno, an architectural mosaic in Czechia's South Moravia region. It's Central Europe's largest sinkhole and part of the Punkevní jeskyně (Punkva Caves), carved out by tributaries of the underground river Punkva. Take a guided tour of its depths, where stalactite-hung chambers look like fanged mouths, or join a motorboat ride through the tunnels. But don't listen to the echoes – it's just the void calling.

IT'S FREE TO view the gorge from the observation platforms at 138m (453ft) and 92m (302ft). Guided tours (daily in summer, or at weekends) of the Punkva Caves take you right down into the abyss.

ITALIAN CHAPEL

An ornate Italian-style chapel, set within two refashioned WWII Nissen huts, is now a symbol of reconciliation on wind-blasted Lamb Holm, one of Scotland's Orkney Islands.

In 1942, Italian prisoners of war were brought to work on causeways linking Orkney to the southern islands. When Italy capitulated in 1943, they were prisoners no more. They lobbied for a place of worship, and were soon using every spare hour transforming the huts: lining the walls, painting frescoes and moulding a font out of concrete. The chapel's elaborate decorations are all the more remarkable, considering wartime constraints on building materials. Its interior has a womblike ambience, with a rosy brick-built vault framing an altar decorated with the Virgin Mary and cherubs.

● **LAMB HOLM IS** a short drive from Orkney's capital, Kirkwall. The chapel is open daily, but hours vary.

SAARLAND, GERMANY

VÖLKLINGER HÜTTE

Imagine the cacophonous clanking of an industrial-age ironworks: crackling furnaces, hollering workers and the ringing sound of beaten metal. This blast-furnace complex in Völklingen, Germany, is the only surviving snapshot of Europe's 19th-century iron-making heyday. It quickly grew into the country's biggest production site for steel beams, and its fast-paced production was a blueprint for factories around Europe. During both world wars, prisoners of war were forced to toil here (and were given the most perilous jobs).

UNESCO's World Heritage List more often features palaces and churches than forests of scaffolding and rusty pipes, but Völklinger Hütte graces the list, thanks to its perfectly preserved industrial innovations, like the suspended conveyor belt system. And, like so many retirees, the ironworks has found a new artistic lease of life: today, the factory complex is a museum, gallery space and the venue for the Urban Art Biennale, giving a steampunk setting to cutting-edge contemporary art.

● **LESS THAN TWO** hours by road from Frankfurt (or Strasbourg, across the border in France), the ironworks is open daily. It's well worth timing your visit for a concert or special exhibition.

LONDON'S ODDEST SIGHTS

The UK's capital is practically defined by eccentricity, and even the best-known attractions have peculiar legends attached – whether it's the ghostly carriage of Hyde Park or the Tower of London's guardian ravens. But to hear stories less told about London's oft-forgotten communities, you need to head to small-scale sights – like unhallowed cemeteries, uncommon art galleries and Roman-era ruins.

WALTHAMSTOW

1. GOD'S OWN JUNKYARD

Winking lights, rainbow-coloured bulbs, lipstick-pink lettering and saucy silhouettes create a carnivalesque atmosphere at this showcase of works by the artist Chris Bracey, the luminous mind behind many of Soho's neon signs. Walking through this glowing gallery is an instant mood boost, as well as a colourful glimpse into past decades of Soho's titillating nightlife.

WEST END

2. SOHO NOSES

From 1996 to 2005, artist Rick Buckley secreted up to 35 plaster noses, casts of his own, around Soho. The project is thought to be a statement about the nosiness of London's widespread CCTV cameras. Seek out the seven or so that remain via a guided tour.

Queen
of
Diamonds
CINEMA
PLAY
BELIE

ALICE AYRES
JOHN CRANMER
CAMBRIDGE
AGED 23
G GARNIS
SOLOMAN GALAMAN
JAMES BANNIST

3

IN
LOVING
MEMORY OF
MUFFIN
AGED 15 YEARS

6

7

8

LONDON'S ODDEST SIGHTS

ALDERSGATE

3. THE MEMORIAL TO HEROIC SELF-SACRIFICE

Near St Paul's Cathedral, Postman's Park holds a memorial that's humble in size but mighty in moral stature: ordinary people's extraordinary acts of heroism are inscribed in ceramic tiles along a wall. Stroll a while and consider what history remembers and forgets.

FARRINGDON

4. CHARTERHOUSE PLAGUE PIT

Dig anywhere in London and you risk unearthing a hidden cemetery. Excavations for a railway tunnel unearthed the largest Black Death plague pit at Charterhouse Square, repository of the (thankfully noncontagious) remains of 50,000 people.

BLOOMSBURY

5. EISENHOWER AIR-RAID SHELTER

Eight London Tube stations had deep air-raid shelters during WWII – including this pill-box-shaped building on Chenies St, used by US Army Signal Corps in the run-up to D-Day.

HYDE PARK

6. PET CEMETERY

This pint-sized cemetery, established in Hyde Park in 1881, is the final resting place of beloved Buddys and Fidos. The first stone laid here is engraved with 'Poor Cherry', in memory of a terrier.

BAYSWATER

7. FAKE HOUSES OF LEINSTER GARDENS

Number 23 and 24 Leinster Gdns are not what they seem. Walk around the corner to Porchester Tce and you'll see they're just a facade, built to preserve architectural integrity after demolitions during construction of the Metropolitan Line in the 1860s.

SOUTHWARK

8. CROSS BONES GRAVEYARD

Corpses considered too unseemly for holy ground, such as prostitutes, were buried here. This resting place near Borough Station is now a monument to London's outsiders.

SOHO

9. BROAD STREET WATER PUMP

In 1854, a cholera epidemic in the capital was halted simply by turning off a tap. A replica pump at the corner of Lexington St and Broadwick St marks where John Snow traced the outbreak and removed the handle.

CITY OF LONDON

10. LONDON MITHRAEUM

In 1954, the remains of a Temple of Mithras were discovered in the heart of London's financial district. Town planners were undeterred and simply relocated the ruins nearby, under what's now Bloomberg's European HQ, near Bank Station.

POSTOJNA CAVES

When unearthly amphibians were first seen in Postojna's caves in the 17th century, the obvious explanation was that they were infant dragons. But the truth about the newt-like proteus is almost as intriguing – this ghostly pale amphibian is found only in Postojna's 24km (15 miles) of caves. The hardy proteus (*Proteus anguinus*; also called an olm) can survive up to a decade without food and is completely blind, darting among the subterranean waterways using its ability to perceive weak electrical fields.

The caves and their slimy residents have been welcoming visitors for some time. Miniature trains have trundled into the grotto for more than 140 years: Empress Elisabeth of Austria even took a tour, though sadly the velvet sedan chairs used for her visit are no longer available. Today, the cave walls drip with multi-tentacled stalactites, and pillars of limestone rise like the altar of a baroque cathedral. The shiny 5m/16ft-tall stalagmite dubbed 'The Brilliant' inspires the clicking of cameras, though it's the tanks of proteus that steal the limelight. Biologists have high hopes for what these slippery creatures may contribute to science; their regenerative powers may hold keys to cancer therapies or even slowing down the ageing process in humans. It was only in 2016 that scientists were finally able to observe baby proteus hatching and growing. For now, the baby dragons are keeping their secrets under wraps.

* **POSTOJNA IS AN** hour by bus from the Slovenian capital, Ljubljana.

LYGNSTØYLVATNET

Travellers to Norway are usually hypnotised by soaring cliffs and glassy fjords. But there are wonders beneath the water, too: an entire town lurks beneath Lygnstøylvatnet. In 1908, an avalanche from Mt Keipen set rocky rubble in motion to create a natural dam. The resulting lake, Lygnstøylvatnet, swallowed up huts, bridges, part of a forest and a section of old road. Today, skilled divers don their thickest wetsuits to plunge into the chilly waters, where they can somersault among old stone walls and duck beneath a short bridge, now hemmed by clouds of algae.

* **THE LAKE IS** only for experienced divers and most easily visited by car. A trip is best teamed with a visit to Sunnylven Church and Hellesylt Waterfalls, 35km (22 miles) southeast by road.

LOOPGRAAFBRUG

It's easy to imagine that you are parting the waters as you stride along the 'Moses Bridge' near Halsteren. Walking the length of the sunken pedestrian pathway, also known as the Loopgraafbrug (trench bridge), you'll see that the water rises waist-height on each side. The walkway descends down a muddy bank before burrowing across the moat of Fort de Roovere, an entrenchment that fell to the French during the Austrian War of Succession in the 18th century. RO&AD Architecten masterminded this wooden structure to retain the fortress' austere, isolated air. These days the fort is an under-loved tourist destination, although the bridge itself attracts plenty of curious visitors.

* **FORT DE ROOVERE** is a 100km (62 mile) drive west from Eindhoven, along the A58.

GARNI GORGE

Less than an hour east from Armenia's capital, Yerevan, lies one of the country's most spectacular natural wonders, Garni Gorge. This magnificent geological site is famed for its towering hexagonal and pentagonal basalt columns, as well as a 2000-year-old temple and a UNESCO World Heritage–listed monastery.

Also fondly called the Symphony of Stones, Garni Gorge's dramatic rockfaces resemble the pipes of a massive organ. Shaped by volcanic activity millions of years ago, the uniquely upright shapes were formed when fast-moving lava flows rapidly cooled and hardened under immense pressure. Wind and rain further eroded the soft rock, moulding the orderly pentagonal and hexagonal columns seen today – some so perfect and symmetrical that they look almost human-made. A walkway near the Azat Bridge offers the best closeups of these formations, some towering up to 50m (164ft) high.

While not as ancient as these stone formations, equally striking historic structures are found near and within the scenic gorge. Garni Temple, a pillared Roman-style temple first constructed in 77 CE, overlooks the valley and was rebuilt in the mid-20th century after years of destruction. Another worthwhile sight is Geghard Monastery, dating back to Armenia's earliest days of Christianity, with its main stone church, Surp Astvatsatsin, erected in 1215.

IN YEREVAN, TOUR vehicles line up around Republic Sq with good-value trips to Garni Gorge and other sites beyond the city, though without any guide information. Pay for a pricier tour if you want a guide.

HAUTERIVES, FRANCE

LE PALAIS IDÉAL

Resembling the most extravagant of Hindu temples, the 'Ideal Palace' was built by postal-worker-turned-artist Ferdinand Cheval over a period of 33 years. When his foot struck a pebble on a spring day in 1879, Cheval was inspired by the shape of the rock and pocketed it for safekeeping. He continued picking up unusual pebbles along his 29km (18 miles) postal route, and the collection expanded, becoming the building materials for a fairy-tale palace. Drawing inspiration from a range of eras, Cheval crafted gargoyles, gateways, stairs, turrets and elaborate columns. The palace was completed in 1912 but it was decades later, long after Cheval's death, that visitors began to come to this temple to human patience.

★ THE PALACE IS in Hauterives, 55km (34 miles) south of Lyon.

THE ALPS, SWITZERLAND

TRIFTBRÜCKE

Don't look down: you're walking along one of the Swiss Alps' longest and highest pedestrian bridges, and it's beginning to tremble in a sudden high wind. Even the cable-car ascent to the Triftbrücke seems designed to make your stomach lurch. Built in 2009, the Triftbrücke was modelled after the Nepalese-style triple-rope bridge, a simple but durable design seen across the country's mountain passes. For many walkers, this crossing seems much longer than its 170m (558ft), dangling above the cliffs of the Trift Gorge and dropping to the teal waters of Triftsee. To avoid glancing down, fix your gaze on the panorama of glacier and mountain ahead.

★ THE BRIDGE IS open June to October only. Take the cable car from Nessental Triftbahn bus stop, then a 1½-hour hike each way.

SINGING TREES

Plenty of gardeners sing to their plants, but in Aalborg the plants sing back. Trees in Kildeparken have their own individual soundtracks, often linked to the artist who planted them. This Danish city has been persuading stars to plant trees in Kildeparken since 1987, starting with Cliff Richard. A dazzling roll-call followed his example, including Sting, Beyoncé, Elton John, Shakira and the members of ZZ Top. It seemed logical for Kildeparken to sing its gratitude, so in 2012, oak and cherry trees were wired to play music. Stroll through the park, press the 'play' buttons on the trees, and be serenaded by a choir of tree-hugging celebs.

● **LISTEN TO THE** Singing Trees year-round in Kildeparken, south of central Aalborg near the city's bus and train stations.

CAMPANILE DI CURON

With its backdrop of mountains and forested shores, Reschensee is a snapshot of pristine nature – until you notice a bell tower jutting from the water. This lake in Italy's South Tyrol region was created artificially by the construction of a dam in 1950, merging three lakes into one. Along with 5 sq km (1.9 sq miles) of farmland and dozens of homes, a 14th-century church was forever submerged by the water – except for its bell tower. In midwinter when the lake freezes over, it's possible to walk out to the tower. Arguably the church is even lovelier as an apparition, rising silently from Reschensee.

● **CLOSE TO ITALY'S** border with Switzerland and Austria, the lake is visitable from all three countries.

SARAJEVO, BOSNIA & HERCEGOVINA

SARAJEVO ROSES

Sorrow and hope blossom out of the concrete in Bosnia & Hercegovina's capital. Scars left by deadly mortar strikes during the Siege of Sarajevo have been filled with red resin, creating memorials to the lost. Between 1992 and 1996, more than 300 bombs per day hit the city, launched by Republika Srpska army tanks in the surrounding hills. Over 1425 bloody days, 11,541 civilians were killed here.

When a mortar shell hits a hard surface, it creates a central crater surrounded by smaller dents. When filled with red resin, these markings resemble vivid red blooms – or pools of blood – on Sarajevo's streets. No single person or group claims to have created Sarajevo's roses, so they are deemed to belong to the people who lived through the siege. But as a result, these rose-shaped memorials are bereft of an authority to preserve them. As years passed and sections of road were replaced, many roses disappeared; groups of volunteers now painstakingly repaint those remaining to protect them from footfall and weather damage.

With so many locals carrying physical and psychological scars from the war, the roses' resemblance to open wounds is apt. Though some have mixed feelings about the attention the roses receive from visitors to the city, many more see them as an embodiment of grief and even hope sprouting around Sarajevo.

SARAJEVO ROSES CAN be seen around the city. Look for them at Markale Market, Ferhadija Promenade and Grand Park.

IDRIJA, SLOVENIA
MERCURY MINE

The town of Idrija built its fortune from 500 years of mining poisonous liquid metal. For centuries, mercury was pivotal to technological innovations in thermometers and lamps. Idrija's abundant mercury was discovered in 1490, and the Slovenian town held the world's largest mercury mine for centuries. Down Anthony Mine Shaft, the tunnels have been preserved and the walls still sparkle with beads of the toxic metal (mercifully contained behind glass). The mine is named after the patron saint of miners, and tours bypass a small chapel where workers once prayed before their shifts. Idrija is also famous for its intricate lace, which makes a much more suitable souvenir.

● **IDRIJA IS 60KM** (37 miles) east of Ljubljana. Tours of the mine last 1½ hours.

ZADAR, CROATIA
SEA ORGAN

A lowly melody emanates from the shore in Zadar, trumpeted straight from the bottom of the sea. Here, in the centre of Croatia's glittering coast, a marble staircase conceals the set of 35 pipes and a submerged chamber that comprise the *Sea Organ*. The movement of the waves pushes seawater into the pipes, expelling air tunefully and allowing a melody to waft along the promenade. This sea shanty harnesses the power of the tides. It can be solemn, harmonious or downright atonal, depending on weather conditions or the wake of a passing ferry. This experimental musical artwork was the brainchild of architect Nikola Bašić, and has been piping out its seven mellifluous chords since 2005.

● **THE SEA ORGAN** bellows its melody on the western edge of Zadar's Riva, 500m (1640ft) northwest of the national museum.

EASTERN EUROPE'S RUINS & CULTURAL RELICS

LITHUANIA, POLAND, HUNGARY, ROMANIA & BULGARIA

Eastern Europe is diverse in languages and cultures, but travellers will notice a few uniting themes. Hospitality is abundant, but humour is dark and stoic. Graceful Roman (and pre-Roman) ruins are as common as sites of 20th-century horror, and architectural mood changes are everywhere. Wherever you roam, you'll see up-and-coming art galleries on one corner, and oddball socialist-era monuments on the next.

Even military history buffs who think they have a handle on Eastern Europe's turbulent past will find themselves surprised when they go off the beaten track. Saddle up for Hungarian cowboys, go deep into Cold War subterfuge and see a sparkling side of Poland – you just need an appetite for an epic multi-country drive and zero preconceptions.

TAKE IT SLOWLY. Budget two weeks and break up the very long drives by stopping in small villages and taking side-quests. Start in Vilnius or Kaunas (Lithuania) and finish up in Veliko Târnovo or Plovdiv (Bulgaria) after the final stop.

EASTERN EUROPE'S RUINS & CULTURAL RELICS

COLD WAR MUSEUM, *NEAR PLUNGĖ, LITHUANIA*

Deep amid Žemaitija National Park, a warren of Cold War history snakes beneath concrete domes. The Plokštinė nuclear missile base was a Soviet stronghold built in secrecy; revealed to be a missile launch site in 1978, it now houses a history museum.

ALONG THE WAY: The birch-lined shores of the Curonian Spit, and Šiauliai's Hill of Crosses (p184), are worthy detours; they're both roughly 1½ hours' drive from the base.

NEON MUSEUM, *WARSAW, POLAND*

In dazzling defiance of 1950s Cold War gloom, the Polish School of Posters channelled oppressed creativity into a golden era of design. Bold poster layouts, Art Nouveau fonts and fizzing neon signs are displayed at the glittering Neon Museum – as much a psychedelic daydream as a trip down memory lane for Poles.

ALONG THE WAY: Before crossing into Poland, take in the unsettling variety of demons and witches at Kaunas' eclectic Museum of Devils.

HORTOBÁGY NATIONAL PARK, *EASTERN HUNGARY*

If 'cowboy country' makes you picture the USA's wide open plains, adjust your perceptions: Hungary's *puszta* (plains) have been the stomping ground of cowboys since nomads arrived to graze cattle in the Carpathian Basin some 2000 years ago. From April to October, 800 sq km (309 sq miles) of marshes and pastures come alive with stock herders and horsemen.

ALONG THE WAY: Break up the drive over a couple of days, stopping for Gothic architecture in Slovak cities Bardejov and Košice.

SARMIZEGETUSA REGIA, *TRANSYLVANIA, ROMANIA*

A circular sanctuary of standing stones, a sundial and foundation blocks are all that remain of a city whose story abruptly ended in 106 CE. The kingdom of Dacia ruled for centuries, with Sarmizegetusa Regia as a strategic capital until the Romans tore it down; today you'll have to squint to imagine the former glory of a fortress that once spanned 30,000 sq metres (323,000 sq ft).

ALONG THE WAY: The city of Alba Iulia is a worthy stop, 1½ hours' drive before you reach Sarmizegetusa Regia.

BUZLUDZHA UFO, *CENTRAL MOUNTAINS, BULGARIA*

Glaring down from a 1441m (4727ft) peak, this concrete dome looks ready to beam up hikers in Bulgaria's Central Mountains. Dubbed the 'Buzludzha UFO', it was once an assembly hall. Restoration began on the site's mosaics and roof in 2020, but until the works are complete it remains a romantic wreck. A potholed road zigzags 20km (12 miles) up to the UFO from Shipka village.

ALONG THE WAY: Finish up in Veliko Tarnovo's fortresses or perhaps the Roman ruins of Plovdiv. Both have outdoor cafe scenes to toast your journey's end.

PREVIOUS PAGE: A cowboy canters across Hungary's Hortobágy plains THIS PAGE: The ruins of Sarmizegetusa Regia in Romania's Orastie Mountains

ALBANIA'S CONCRETE BUNKERS

Nothing sums up Albania's bizarre 20th-century history more than its famous bunkers. When I first visited the country more than 20 years ago, these remnants of communist-era paranoia were everywhere. Their domed concrete roofs and narrow eye-slits crouched suggestively on either side of the road to Tirana, ready for an invasion that never came.

Back then, my Albanian friends reacted with something approaching disgust when I said I wanted to go inside one. During Albania's difficult times, the bunkers had been repurposed in various ways – from makeshift toilets to winter stables for goats. But a few years ago, I stumbled across the perfect bunker: in mint condition, defending a bridge over a wide gorge on a backwater road in southern Albania. I slid in through the narrow sniper hole and found the interior pristine, save for evidence of a few birds that had nested there. It was damp inside, a cool refuge from the summer heat, though I didn't find myself envying the soldier who had been billeted there.

Legend has it that Albania's communist dictator Enver Hoxha made the designer of a bunker stand inside the prototype while a tank drove over it. When the bunker's roof survived, the dictator gave the order to cover the entire country in them. It's deliciously ironic, then, that Hoxha's very own bunker near Tirana is now a gallery-museum. Hoxha saw art purely as a vehicle to further political ends – cue Albanian Socialist Realism, with its paintings of patriotic workers and their stern leaders – and he punished artists he deemed anti-conformist. But today, Hoxha's hideout is BUNK'ART 1, which shines a light on life under his regime. Meanwhile in the heart of Tirana, BUNK'ART 2 exposes the regime's horrors. Within, find displays about Albania's tens of thousands of political prisoners, along with troves of letters of dissent against Hoxha – the country's secrets finally brought to light. –*TOM MASTERS*

★ **BUNK'ART 2 IS** five minutes' walk south of Tirana's Palace of Culture. To reach BUNK'ART 1, take a Linzë-bound bus.

WITCHES' HILL

If you do decide to go down to the woods today, you might see devils and warty witches glaring through the birch trees. On the Curonian Spit, the narrow tendril of land connecting Lithuania with the Russian territory of Kaliningrad, sinister folkloric wood carvings speckle a forested sand dune. Raganų Kalnas (Witches' Hill) is an open-air sculpture gallery comprising 71 charmingly creepy figures from the Neringa region, whittled from wood between 1979 and the early 2000s. This enigmatic glade, an easy 20km (12 miles) drive south from the port town of Klaipėda, has hosted midsummer folk celebrations for centuries. You'll find satanic totem poles, toothy dragons and a tiny playground where you can slide down a crone's tongue.

● **RAGANŲ KALNAS IS** clearly signposted from the main road in Juodkrantė.

LINDHOLM HØJE

It should come as no surprise that one of the most important pieces of Aalborg's historical heritage is tied to the Vikings. Scattered across a hilltop pasture and ringed by a wall of beech trees, the burial ground of Lindholm Høje marks one of Scandinavia's most spectacular (and eerie) archaeological sites, holding nearly 700 graves from the Iron Age and Viking Age. Many of the graves are marked by stones arranged in a distinctive outline of a ship.

Around 1000 CE, drifting sand covered the area, preserving it until its discovery in modern times. Excavations began in the late 19th century and revealed many valuable insights into Viking life. Lindholm Høje Museet adjoins the site and dives into its history, including a tragic fire that engulfed a farm more than 2000 years ago.

● **LOCATED NORTH OF** Aalborg, Lindholm Høje is reachable via a 15-minute bus ride from the city centre.

IL-MAQLUBA

On the Mediterranean island of Malta, just outside Qrendi village, the apricot-coloured ground suddenly gives way. Locals named this yawning sinkhole Il-Maqluba – literally 'the overturned' or 'upside down' in Maltese – and it has the appearance of an English country garden on Mars. The crater's burnt sienna rim is tangled with gum and carob trees, and the limestone walls are dressed in ivy.

The 50m/164ft-diameter crater opened up when an earthquake in 1343 caused a limestone shelf to crumble. But the Maltese prefer its supernatural origin story: angels scooped up giant handfuls of the land and cast them into the sea as a punishment for villagers' sins. This angelic act of vandalism is said to have left behind the gaping 15m/49ft-deep sinkhole and also created the islet of Filfla, 4.5km (2.8 miles) off the southwest coast. The myth has a faint echo of the truth: tiny Filfla was indeed broken off from the rest of Malta, but probably as a result of tectonic stresses within the Maghlaq fault zone. And rather than being the result of *divine* punishment, Filfla had to endure British Royal Air Force target practice until the bombardments fell silent in 1971. Today only screaming shearwaters and gulls pierce the silence.

When you arrive at Il-Maqluba, peer right over the crater's edge; the ground drops abruptly and you can stroll partway down on a viewing area. At night the tunnels, carved out by groundwater, are homes for long-eared bats and other endemic creatures.

● **THE VILLAGE OF** Qrendi is barely five minutes' drive from Malta International Airport. Il-Maqluba is free to visit. Don't descend all the way to the bottom of the sinkhole; follow signs to the belvedere only.

UUNARTOQ ISLAND, GREENLAND

UUNARTOQ HOT SPRINGS

No one has fallen for the name 'Greenland' since the Norsemen. When wayfaring 10th-century explorer Erik the Red bestowed this name, it was an attempt at good PR: he wanted to attract more settlers by implying that Greenland was a place of ease and plenty. Of course, Greenland is not very green – in fact, it's 80% ice sheet – but balmy corners do exist, especially on little Uunartoq Qeqertaq (Warming Island).

Uunartoq has no permanent population and never has; no wonder tales swirl about the spirits inhabiting the sea mist. Fortunately this didn't deter Norsemen from exploring it and discovering, to their delight, a rare hot spring.

There are thousands of natural springs welling up across Greenland, but Uunartoq has the only known one that's consistently warm enough to bathe in. Three thermal springs flow into a small pool that's heated by the immense friction between rocky layers underground. The waters remain a toe-toasting, shoulder-unhunching 38°C (100°F), and the sight of icebergs bobbing along the shore makes the warmth all the more delicious.

The ferry to the island, with the possibility of whale sightings, adds to the feeling of being at one with the wilderness. This is a simple place with no amenities, leaving nothing between you and nature; just perfectly clear water, a backdrop of snow-streaked mountains and the comforting warmth of Mother Earth's rumbles.

● BOATS TO UUNARTOQ depart from Qaqortoq, which is a 1¼-hour flight from the capital city of Nuuk (road connections in Greenland are few). Tours operate in summer.

CHERNOBYL EXCLUSION ZONE

"**D**on't touch the moss!" bellowed my guide. In the Chernobyl Exclusion Zone, background radiation is 10 times the normal level – and slow-growing plants like moss absorb it like a sponge.

On 26 April 1986, an attempted safety-system test at Chernobyl Nuclear Power Plant unleashed the worst nuclear disaster ever seen, ranked 7 on the International Nuclear Event Scale (there is no 8). An explosion ripped through Reactor 4, releasing radioactive particles into the air that were swept as far as the UK and Scandinavia. The town of Pripyat had been purpose-built for plant workers, and its population of some 50,000 were among those bussed away from their homes, never to return.

Pripyat is now a freeze-frame of Soviet Ukraine. Its Ferris wheel and playground, built shortly before the accident, stand as rusty symbols of lost innocence. In apartment blocks, creeper plants drag at the walls and stairwells decay. Mouldering schoolbooks, upturned desks and child-sized gas masks litter the floor of its school. Reactor 4 was hurriedly enclosed in a concrete sarcophagus, and later entombed in the multilayered 'New Safe Confinement' structure.

When I first visited the exclusion zone in 2010, I was expecting a landscape laid waste by nuclear disaster, devoid of wildlife. But as I stepped gingerly across Pripyat's confetti-coating of broken glass almost 25 years after the disaster, I kicked more than one empty vodka bottle from my path – detritus from illicit parties in the exclusion zone. Birdlife was chattering from the trees and trees were bursting from abandoned buildings. Nature appeared to be doing just fine, in spite of humankind's brushes with disaster.

But danger continues to rain down: in February 2025, a Russian warhead struck the power plant's protective shell. Seeing smoke pour from Chernobyl's nuclear power plant instantly rekindled Ukrainians' worst memories of 1986, but to the relief of all of Europe, the New Safe Confinement structure sealing in the reactor remained intact. Later that year, Ukraine's president, Volodymyr Zelenskyy, accused Russia of deploying drones to cut power to the decommissioned plant – a chilling reminder of how Chernobyl, and its barely contained powers of destruction, still looms large. —*ANITA ISALSKA*

* **AT THE TIME** of writing, travel was not advised to Ukraine.

PÚBOL, SPAIN

CASTELL DE PÚBOL

Referring to Gala Dalí merely as the wife of Salvador doesn't do justice to this formidable woman, muse of some of the 20th century's greatest artists. The Castell de Púbol was her retreat from Salvador Dalí's whirlwind existence, and it offers teasing insights into the shared life of surrealism's most famous couple.

Russian-born Gala married literary giant Paul Éluard and took Dadaist artist Max Ernst as a lover, before moving on to Salvador Dalí. They married, though Gala's dalliances didn't stop. In fact, the prospect of his charismatic wife playing away was thrilling to Salvador. Besotted with Gala, he was delighted by the idea of giving her a place to 'reign like an absolute sovereign'. In 1969, he bought a medieval castle in Púbol, decorating it according to Gala's tastes. Orna-menting the Gothic-meets-Renaissance chateau with antiques and hand-painted ceilings was a labour of love. Velvet drapes and candelabra still decorate its walls, while a lip-shaped sofa and fountains with angler-fish statues add dashes of surreality. Gala would only allow Salvador permission to visit Castell de Púbol if he submitted a handwritten request.

The palace eventually became Gala's tomb. After her burial in its basement, Salvador used the castle as an artist's studio, hoping to channel his muse from the beyond.

● **VISIT BY CAR** or tour, or via a bus to La Pera. Castell de Púbol opens mid-March to mid-January.

ŞINCA, ROMANIA
ŞINCA VECHE

A beam of sunlight pierces the gloom of the cave. A cluster of devotees, standing with eyes closed, palms outstretched, are bathed in light. They represent only a few of the spiritual seekers who journey to Şinca Veche's cave temple. Although it was established by monks in the 1700s, the site's spiritual significance is thought to date back much earlier. Its main chamber resembles a garden shed, with planks of wood and a cross marking a sandy entryway. Within, candles flicker around makeshift altars, while light streams through an opening in the cave roof. Locals whisper that praying here heals fertility problems. From the cave mouth, paths lead to a small, immaculate hermitage and gardens.

● **THE TEMPLE STANDS** 1km (0.6 miles) south of Şinca Veche; you'll need your own transport. It's an easy detour between Sibiu and Braşov.

COUNTY KERRY, IRELAND
BEEHIVE HUTS

Like sheep and country pubs, *clochán* (beehive huts) are familiar features of the landscape along southwest Ireland's coast. Dozens of these dry-stone constructions are scattered across the emerald-green hills – throwbacks to an agrarian, and perhaps spiritual, past. Historians date these squat shelters, which slightly resemble round medieval helmets, back to the 8th century CE. Their dry-stone walls are as girthy as 1.5m (4.9ft) thick, assembled through corbelling, where overlapping stones act as counterweights to one another and hold the entire structure together. Seek them out in sea-spray-slapped coastal Fahan.

Step inside a *clochán* to be temporarily cocooned from the wind; they're thought to have been used for grain storage or as shelters against sudden storms. Historians theorise that they may even have served as suitably austere temporary dwellings for monks and pilgrims making their way to the summit of Cnoc Bréanainn (Brendan's Hill, named for the Irish saint).

● **EMBARK ON A** road trip to see beehive huts, forts and sleepy villages by following the coast around the Dingle Peninsula, four hours' drive from the ferry- and plane-connected Irish capital, Dublin.

GLOBAL SEED VAULT

If you've ever mulled over how humankind could begin anew after a global disaster – say, crop failure or a zombie apocalypse – then you will be heartened to hear about Norway's Global Seed Vault. Squirrelled away on the northerly archipelago of Svalbard, the bank's mission is to store enough seeds to ensure genetic diversity among crops around the globe.

Around 1700 agricultural outposts across the world already carry their own stocks of seeds. Diverse varieties of crops, resistant to disease or hardy in droughts, are stored quietly for a rainy day (or rather, a not-so-rainy one). Their fragile contents would be easily lost in power outages or human-made disasters, so the Global Seed Vault provides the ultimate back-up plan: some 1.3 million samples of around 5000 plant species, safely stashed in sealed baggies within a far-flung Arctic safehouse.

It doesn't get much safer, or more remote, than halfway between northern Norway and the North Pole. The site even has James Bond–esque safeguards in place: in the event of a power failure, the seldom-opened vault will remain sealed so that the permafrost will keep stocks cold. And security measures stipulate that the stored seeds can only be retrieved by the nation that placed them here, ensuring no one can capitalise on another country's agricultural crisis. Unsurprisingly, it's closed to visitors, though you can take a virtual tour via the website (seedvault.no).

IMMERSE IN THE Global Seed Vault's frosty surroundings by exploring Svalbard, reachable by flights from Oslo and Tromsø.

LES GROTTES PÉTRIFIANTES SAVONNIÈRES

You can't rush art – especially when the artist is the Savonnières cave system, where mineral-rich water trickling slowly across the caverns applies a glistening coat to anything in its way. Place any object in the waters of these caves and within a year it will be entirely coated in limestone – but nature needs a helping hand, so items are turned regularly to ensure the resulting 'sculptures' aren't lopsided.

Riddled into the local tuffeau limestone (source material for Loire Valley châteaux such as Chambord), this subterranean system was mostly formed during the Middle Ages. Inside, explore a goblin kingdom of dangling stalactites, overhanging ledges and tiered rock formations. These cool caverns also have exactly the right humidity levels to store wine; the final chamber even offers winetasting.

• THE CAVES ARE 16km (10 miles) west of Tours. Visits (February to November) are by hourlong guided tour.

MUSEUM DR GUISLAIN

Thanks to its brick arches and cathedral windows, Ghent's Museum Dr Guislain is an impressive – if ominous – sight. Belgium's first psychiatric hospital, dating to 1857, houses a museum that is both gruesome and uplifting, taking visitors on a journey through the history of mental health. Freezing water and spinning chambers were among the unpleasant methods of scaring people sane during the late 18th and early 19th century; repress a shudder as you sidle past straightjackets, cages, shackles and radiographic equipment dating to the turn of the 20th century. Then allow your faith to be restored: Joseph Guislain, who established the original hospice here, was a healthcare reformer who helped phase out brutish treatments and pioneered humane, patient-focused care.

• THIS NEOGOTHIC COMPLEX is located 2km (1.2 miles) north of Ghent's Old Town at Jozef Guislainstraat 43; hop aboard tram number 1 to Guislainstraat.

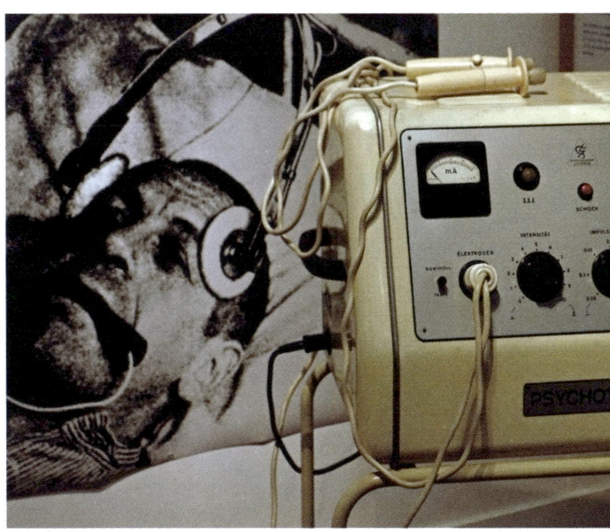

NERVE-RACKING ROCKS

Monumental rocks, cliffs and sinkholes are footprints of the geological past. They remind us how earthquakes birthed mountains, and ancient glaciers carved the land – and how these epic timescales contrast with our own minuscule lifespans. Feel awed by the Earth's eons at these cliff-edge outcrops and precariously balanced boulders.

NEAR TYSSEDAL, NORWAY

1. TROLLTUNGA

The tongue of rock jutting above the water at Ringedalsvatnet is one of Norway's most spectacular photo ops. Hikers embark on a tough, 12-hour circuit from Skjeggedal to reach this panorama of sheer cliffs above water. The highlight is balancing on the 700m/2300ft-high rock, one of several nerve-jangling outcrops you can pose on around the world.

NEAR CHENNAI, INDIA

2. BALANCING ROCK OF MAMALLAPURAM

It's a 250-tonne (276-ton) rock, 6m (20ft) tall and on a 45-degree slope, but attempts to roll 'Krishna's Butterball' downhill have failed, and tourists safely pose beneath.

4

7

8

9

NERVE-RACKING ROCKS

PARQUE NACIONAL DA TIJUCA, BRAZIL

3. PEDRA DA GÁVEA

For a death-defying holiday photo, take a tough six-hour guided hike to this 844m/2769ft-high Rio lookout. From the right angle, you'll appear to cling to a rock high above the beach; in reality, you're two feet from solid ground.

NEAR ØYGARDSTØL, NORWAY

4. KJERAGBOLTEN

Hike a steep route (partially assisted by chains) to assume the ultimate in daring poses atop this boulder, gripped between two cliffs above a 984m (3228ft) drop. The block was deposited here by glacial movement and has become a vertigo-inducing spot for a photo.

NOVA SCOTIA, CANADA

5. NATURE'S TIME POST

Inspiring countless attempts at perspective-trickery photos, and reachable via a 2.5km (1.6 mile) hike (and 235 stairs) south of Tiverton, the basalt column known as 'Nature's Time Post' appears to balance on its tip on the corner of a larger rock in the Bay of Fundy.

NEAR PREIKESTOLHYTTA , NORWAY

6. PREIKESTOLEN

Rising sharply 604m (1982ft) above the Lysefjord, 'Pulpit Rock' is the reward for an intense four-hour hike in Norway's Ryfylke fjord region – snap a photo near the edge, but not *that* near the edge!

NORTHERN TERRITORY, AUSTRALIA

7. DEVIL'S MARBLES

Granite globes are dotted around a parched valley in the Karlu Karlu/Devil's Marbles Conservation Reserve. To Aboriginal people, these weathered boulders and the surrounding landscape have sacred significance. One pair seemingly defy gravity.

OREGON, USA

8. THOR'S WELL

Punched into the dark basalt shoreline, an ominous 6m/20ft-deep cauldron appears to drain the entire ocean away. The rise and fall of the water is dramatic at high tide; see it on a road trip of Oregon's coast along US Rte 101.

ARIZONA, USA

9. CHIRICAHUA NATIONAL MONUMENT

Hike the creeks, volcanic formations and grottoes of this Arizona park to the Big Balanced Rock, perched improbably at its narrow bottom like a spinning top.

RUOKOLAHTI, FINLAND

10. KUMMAKIVI

It's impossible to resist posing, arms raised, beneath this boulder in Finland. Performing a balancing act on a low mound, the 7m/23ft-wide rock was deposited in the forest by glacial movement, though folktales blame trolls.

DOMUS DE JANAS TOMBS

On the island of Sardinia, the ancient dead are keeping their secrets – and their underground tombs are designed to keep restless souls at bay.

Hundreds of hidden tombs – known as the Domus de Janas tombs – are carved into Sardinia's sunbaked limestone. These necropolises and tunnels are the last remnants of the prehistoric Ozieri people, whose farming and hunting culture is thought to have thrived here from the 5th to the 3rd millennium BCE.

The tombs' complex designs continue to confound archaeologists. Their meandering layouts suggest a hierarchical society, in which social orders persisted beyond death. Inside the chambers, walls are awash in crimson patterns and inscribed with mysterious motifs, from spirals and scythes to bull's heads. Most chilling are the false doors, thought to be an attempt to keep the threshold between living and dead firmly closed.

The Ozieri peoples' biggest settlement was at Su Coddu, around 3400 BCE, though this warren of tunnels is now obscured by modern development. Across the centuries, the subterranean passageways attracted various superstitions; while some cultures considered them to be the houses of fairy folk, others pragmatically repurposed them as sheep shelters.

The most impressive tomb discovered so far is the Necropoli di Anghelu Ruju, near Alghero, stumbled upon during construction work at a winery. Excavations of goddess statues, jewellery and arrowheads, dating to 3300 BCE, offer even more tantalising glimpses of this rich, artistic civilisation, now lost to labyrinths below ground.

FERRIES REACH SARDINIA from Genoa and Naples, as well as Barcelona (Spain) and Nice (France). The Necropoli di Anghelu Ruju is 10km (6 miles) north of the northwestern city of Alghero, and is open daily.

KALETO FORTRESS

It's hard to tell where the citadel ends and boulders begin at Belogradchik's fortress, stealthily camouflaged amid rocks on the northerly slopes of the Balkan Mountains. With walls 2m (7ft) thick and 12m (39ft) high, this sturdy stronghold was a key lookout during the medieval Second Bulgarian Empire. Climbing ladders give access to some of the site's most vertiginous outcrops, allowing you to imagine surveying the hills for medieval armies on the move. The rocks whisper their own secrets, too; some have strangely humanoid shapes, giving rise to folktales about their origins. One story describes a beautiful nun who became pregnant but was saved from disgrace by being turned to stone – little comfort, perhaps.

* **KALETO FORTRESS IS** signposted from the town of Belograd-chik in northwestern Bulgaria; it looms 1km (0.6 miles) southwest of the centre.

ŽELÍZY STONE DEVILS

These sinister statues might stop you in your tracks. Like a nightmarish Mt Rushmore, two stone *Čertovy hlavy* (devil heads) lurk on the forested outskirts of Želízy, 35km (22 miles) north of Prague. The creator of these sculptures is Czech artist Václav Levý, a shoemaker's son who rose to prominence as a sculptor. He took his craft as far as Rome and Vienna, and decorated churches across the continent – including the tympanum of mighty St Vitus in Prague. Still, it's a little surprising that a sculptor renowned for religious themes should have left two monstrous visages to gather moss in the Czech countryside.

* **THE DEVILS ARE** on a hillock south of Želízy village, visible from the main road. It's a 300m (984ft) walk from the centre.

CROOKED FOREST

Hansel and Gretel would run in the opposite direction from this unsettling forest, where trees snake out of the ground at an unnatural angle. In the witchy woodland of Krzywy Las – 'Crooked Forest' – more than 400 pine trees have a peculiar C-shaped bend. Theories are wide-ranging: some suggest unusually heavy snowfall could have crushed the trees in this grove while they were saplings; others have said that wartime tanks may have rumbled through and distorted their growth. However, inventive farming methods are the most likely culprit. Curved logs would have been awfully handy for shipbuilding, so experimental farmers may have intervened with the trees' natural growth (though no one has admitted to it).

● **THIS WACKY GLADE** is 2km (1.2 miles) north of Nowe Czarnowo, which is 33km (21 miles) south of Szczecin, a lively port in western Poland.

VENTAS RUMBA

Kuldīga's most celebrated attraction, Ventas Rumba is often affectionately referred to as 'Europe's widest waterfall'. While this title may sound a bit grand for this small 2m (7ft) drop on the Venta River, this zigzagging strip of whitewater is an idyllic sight – and arguably much more captivating when viewed from above. Its understated beauty becomes all the more impressive the longer you look at it and enjoy the rippling waters, the calming sound of tonnes of water cascading over the edge. This scene is best admired from the town's castle hill, on which only a handful of stones from the city's medieval fortress still remain. Today, the hill is home to a park presided over by the Castle Watchman's House that dates back to the mid-1700s. In spring, crowds gather at the falls to watch *vimba* (a type of migratory bream) leap across the falls during their migration.

● **KULDĪGA IS LOCATED** about 154km (96 miles) west of Rīga, easily reachable by bus.

HAUTE-VIENNE, FRANCE

THE MARTYRED VILLAGE OF ORADOUR-SUR-GLANE

Not a single burned-out car was removed after the massacre of Oradour-sur-Glane. The remains of this French village, where 642 civilian residents were killed during WWII, are memorialised as a warning to future generations.

On 10 June 1944, Nazi soldiers entered Oradour-sur-Glane. They divided the villagers between barns and the church, then murdered them. The few surviving eyewitnesses recall that men's legs were shot to prevent escape before they were slaughtered. Women and children were barred inside a church, which was then set on fire, and were shot as they tried to escape. An American navigator who witnessed the aftermath even reported a scene of crucifixion. It was WWII's worst Nazi massacre of French civilians, and historians still wonder why Oradour-sur-Glane was targeted. Retaliation for partisan attacks was common, but this little village was no hotbed of the French Resistance.

After the war, Charles de Gaulle announced the rebuilding of Oradour-sur-Glane northwest of the original village. The charred rubble of the martyred town would be preserved, making it unique among destroyed villages in Europe, most of which were rebuilt on the same spot or marked with memorials. A sign at the entrance reads simply 'Souviens-Toi' (Remember). But remembrance doesn't come easy, especially as the site begins to decay.

● **ORADOUR-SUR-GLANE'S MEMORIAL CENTRE** and village is 20km (12 miles) northwest of Limoges.

WOODEN CHURCHES

The wooden churches of Slovakia's Carpathian Mountains are marvels of artisanship. The majority were built between the 17th and 19th centuries, when they were lovingly carved and filled with painted icons. Most were constructed without using a single nail.

Discovering them is part of the fun: drive among the patchwork of meadows that covers eastern Slovakia, pull over in a sleepy village, and knock on the door of a gingerbread-esque church. Some of the oldest are Gothic in style, such as Hervartov's church, with its distinctive witch's-hat shape; others resemble grand farmhouses with whitewashed walls and wooden eaves, as in Kežmarok.

These sedate villages see few tourists, so you'll have to wait for – or perhaps, indeed, wake – a caretaker to grant you access (their phone numbers are sometimes posted on the doors). Once you strike it lucky and gain entry to one of these intimate shrines, the beauty within is staggering: one of the loveliest is the Greek Catholic church in Jedlinka (built in 1736), harbouring a gloriously gilded iconostasis.

The churches also bear witness to intriguing moments of history. Several were enclaves of peace and tolerance during the anti-Hapsburg revolutions. The denominations represented, including Greek Catholic and Lutheran, are testament to the variety of Christian faiths practised across this region.

● **EXPERIENCE THE WOODEN** churches as part of a road trip.

BAJINA BAŠTA, BOSNIA & HERCEGOVINA

DRINA RIVER HOUSE

Ever grumbled about noisy neighbours or dreamed of having river views? This tiny house is marooned on a rocky islet in the middle of the Drina River – the watery seam that separates Bosnia & Hercegovina and Serbia. Built in the 1960s by locals yearning for some blissful isolation, the photogenic chalet seems to defy gravity on its rocky perch, with barely enough shore space to moor a kayak. Vulnerable to flooding, this pocket-sized hideaway has been rebuilt more than once. These days it's much photographed by visitors to tranquil Bajina Bašta village, and remains a curiosity for canoeists wending their way down the river.

● **BAJINA BAŠTA IS** a quiet spot; you'll need private transport. It's a three-hour drive from Belgrade.

SLOVENSKÝ RAJ NATIONAL PARK, SLOVAKIA

DOBŠINSKÁ ICE CAVE

There is a dark majesty to Slovenský Raj National Park, where bats flutter between limestone cliffs and sinkholes dot the plateaus. Within this Slovakian nature reserve, the phenomenon most guaranteed to elicit a shiver (literally) is Dobšinská Ice Cave. This UNESCO-listed cave is one of the coldest locations in the country: cold air sinks in and warm air can't penetrate its depths, allowing more than 115,000 cu metres (4,061,187 cu ft) of ice to amass here. Frozen walls of ice, as thick as 25m (82ft), gleam blue and silver. Frosty stalactites sparkle from the cave ceiling, and thick pillars of ice seem plucked from a Snow Queen's ballroom. Scientists are monitoring the cave for changes to the ice but, for now, it remains frozen in eternal winter.

● **FROM THE CAR** park, it's a 20-minute walk to the entrance. Guided tours only.

RÍO TINTO

However far we stray from our animal instincts, certain impulses never leave – and that includes avoiding any body of water that's stained bloody red.

The highly acidic 'Red River' in southwestern Spain contains extraordinary levels of heavy metals, and 50 of its kilometres (31 miles) have an ominously rusty hue. Between the Río Tinto's sickly sheen and reddish mountains, the landscape is unequivocally alien. Is it the site of a human-made ecological disaster, or the fault of microorganisms that break down minerals into heavy metal sulphides? Both have played their part: starting with the Romans, this valley has endured 5000 years of mining for precious metals and minerals like gold and copper, with occasional downtime for periods of war or economic decline. In the late 19th century, mining activity intensified under the now-multinational Rio Tinto company, which has racked up environmental criticisms along the way.

Remarkably, life thrives near this troubled waterway. Flamingos dance at the Marismas del Odiel, an altogether cleaner estuary where the Tinto and Odiel rivers meet, along with grebes, plovers and all manner of waterbirds (and, in winter, migratory herons and cranes). But leave joyous abandon to the birds... don't dip a single toe in the red section of the river (staining will be instant), and don't get the water on your face.

● **GET TO THE** bottom of the Río Tinto (not literally!) at the Parque Minero de Riotinto, where you can explore a museum and old miners' house, and trundle by train along 22km (14 miles) of the scenic, mineral-rich landscape.

HILL OF CROSSES

Lithuania's crucifix-covered mound is no humble pilgrimage spot. The Hill of Crosses (Kryžių kalnas) forms a defiant, spiky silhouette that grew from protests against Soviet oppression.

Locals have laid crosses here since the 19th century; it's thought that the first honoured were those who died during an anti-tsarist uprising. A total of 130 were counted in 1900, and they continued to be laid for decades thereafter. Soviet authorities tried to stop this public display of devotion by bulldozing the site in 1961; wooden crosses were burnt and metallic ones melted. But this only spurred on the faithful, who crept in and added more crosses under a cloak of darkness. The KGB tried every trick in the book, from roadblocks to marking the area as a quarantine zone. Nothing worked: the hill grew higher, crucifix by crucifix.

After 1989, when Lithuania struggled free from the Iron Curtain, the hill became a symbol of victory. Crosses were laid here openly, from simple bound twigs to ornate silver ones, and memorials honouring those deported to Siberia under the Soviets. Pope John Paul II's 1993 visit solidified the site's status as a pilgrimage spot, and the hill bulged to 60m (197ft) long and almost as wide. The current number of crosses is estimated at 100,000 and counting.

* **THE HILL OF** Crosses is 12km (7.5 miles) north of Šiauliai. Drive or take a Joniškis-bound bus.

LIVING FIRES

The plains of Lopătari are an infernal wasteland, where a sulphurous stench fills the air and flames burst from the soil. Fortunately, the so-called 'living fire' (*focul viu* in Romanian) only rises to 20cm (8in) in height. Natural gases rather than demonic influence produce the blazes, which smoulder away within cracks in the dark earth. At night, when the plains are speckled with orange and blue fire, the land has a truly hellish air. But Romanian folklore's account of the living fires is rather cheering, explaining them as purifying flames that protect wildlife and bestow good fortune. However, singed shoes aren't considered lucky, so watch your step.

● **DRIVE THE DJ203K** road for approximately 60km (37 miles) from Buzău towards Terca, ideally with a 4WD (the road is rough). Handwritten signs direct the final hike to the fires.

KIJK-KUBUS MUSEUM-HOUSE

Rotterdam is replete with innovative architectural marvels, but one building stands out – the higgledy-piggledy-tilted yellow-and-grey cubes of the Overblaak Development, designed by Piet Blom. Each of these 'cube houses' was built to resemble a tree, so the collective effect is that of a forest. Visitors can tour one of the buildings at the Kijk-Kubus Museum-House. You might expect your head to spin with disorientation as you're led upside down or at odd inclines, but the 45-degree angles you see outside the building are completely at odds with the logical interior. However, there is a need for customised angular furniture to fit the quirky dimensions.

● **KIJK-KUBUS IS OPPOSITE** Rotterdam Blaak station, and opens 11am to 6pm daily.

NORTH AMERICA

THIS PAGE: A lighthouse crowns sandstone cliffs in the Apostle Islands, USA (p206)

THE GLASS HOUSE

If you were an undertaker, what would you do with the thousands of glass bottles of embalming fluid left over from preserving a career's worth of dead bodies? Well, if you're Canadian funeral director David H Brown, you build your house with them.

My windscreen wipers are working overtime as I drive north through eastern British Columbia, searching for this oddity known as the Glass House. The drenching rain blurs views of Kootenay Lake and the wooded hills. Patches of fog along the snaking treelined road give it a slightly sinister start-of-a-horror-movie air, though perhaps that's just my imagination.

Brown constructed his Glass House in the 1950s from more than 500,000 empty embalming fluid bottles. After retiring, he decided that this funeral-industry byproduct could be put to good use, and set about collecting discarded bottles from funeral homes across western Canada to build his woodland cottage.

When I pull in at the Glass House, set in forested gardens overlooking Kootenay Lake, I'm surprised to find a fairy-tale castle, with turrets, rounded walls and rectangular merlons jutting up from the roof. The exterior appears to be made from thousands of square glass bricks and, even on this grey day, it sparkles. Bright red paint trims the cross-hatched windows, flowers bloom along stone ledges, and vividly painted, oddly lifelike gnomes peek out from under the bushes.

The interior of the 111-sq-metre (1195-sq-ft) house is more pedestrian, preserved as it was 50 years ago. An old sewing machine sits atop a wooden table, a vintage baby carriage on a braided rug nearby. The pine-panelled kitchen has yellowing Formica counters and a white Frigidaire stove. The only hint that this house isn't a typical 1950s suburban bungalow is a display of photos detailing its construction, depicting walls of glass rising between the pines.

In the garden, it's a fairyland again, with bridges and paths through the woods incorporating more of the bottles. A testament to one man's weirdly compelling vision, the Glass House was David Brown's dream home. To him, using the byproducts of his industry wasn't eerie, but sensible, practical, even a bit fanciful. Cute garden gnomes and all. *–CAROLYN B HELLER*

THE GLASS HOUSE, 11341 Hwy 3A, is just south of Boswell and 40km (25 miles) north of Creston in BC. It's open daily for tours from May to October.

UKRAINIAN CULTURAL HERITAGE VILLAGE

Out in the towns and grasslands of eastern Alberta, beacons of Ukrainian culture entice curious motorists to pull over. In Glendon, a 2700kg (6000lb) dumpling statue is the focal point for an annual food festival; while in Vegreville, a 9m/30ft-long *pysanka* (decorated Easter egg) dazzles with 524 stars. But the nucleus of this flourishing eastern European diaspora is the Ukrainian Cultural Heritage Village.

"Visiting the village is like stepping into a living time capsule," enthuses Pam Trischuk, its head of education and interpretation. "You can hear the chickens, ride the wagon, walk the dusty roads and smell food cooking, and you really feel the rural lifestyles as they were lived by the early Ukrainian settlers."

Starting in the early 1890s, Ukrainians began emigrating to eastern Alberta, leaving behind the Austro-Hungarian crown lands of Galicia and Bukovina to farm Canada. The village's traditional houses and restored buildings paint a vivid picture of early settler life.

"One of my favourite buildings is our 1920s grain elevator," says Trischuk. "It tells a really powerful story: the role of agriculture in Alberta's history and how Ukrainian settlers really helped to feed Alberta – and even the rest of the world."

Today, roughly 20% of Alberta's population have Ukrainian origin, but they aren't the only ones rocking up at the village. "Non-Ukrainian visitors are often surprised at how relatable and universal the stories of early Ukrainian settlers are," says Trischuk. "We talk about migration, resilience, building a new life, cultural traditions, connection across generations. And those resonate with everyone."

THE VILLAGE IS 50km (31 miles) east of Edmonton. A grassfire caused damage in April 2025, but mercifully left historic buildings intact. The village remained closed for the remainder of that year but at the time of writing, planned to reopen again the following season in summer 2026.

OREGON, USA

THE GIANT PUMPKIN REGATTA

Humankind has accomplished many feats throughout the course of history: mastering fire, developing agriculture and landing on the moon. But few compare to carving out a humongous pumpkin and using it as a boat.

The West Coast Giant Pumpkin Regatta in Tualatin is the culmination of aeons of human engineering – and it's hilarious. After carving out the centres of giant pumpkins, paddlers don fancy-dress costumes and race across a lake towards glory. Not particularly known for their seaworthiness, the pumpkins bounce and bob across the water – and sometimes the paddler manages to stay inside. An associated festival also features a giant-pumpkin weigh-off, best-costume prizes, a pie-eating contest and tons more.

● **THE FESTIVAL IS** held every October in Tualatin, just south of Portland, Oregon.

ARIZONA, USA

METEOR CRATER

Around 50,000 years ago, a meteor blazed through the atmosphere and smacked into the middle of the high desert, creating what is arguably Arizona's second-most impressive pit (after the Grand Canyon, of course). Meteor Crater, also called Barringer Crater, is an out-of-this-world site that some experts say is the most well-preserved meteorite impact on Earth. Reaching around 1200m (3937ft) in diameter and 170m (558ft) deep, the crater can be admired from multiple viewpoints around the rim. While hiking to the bottom is not allowed, exhibits at the amusing yet informative visitor center is well worth the visit to learn more about this mind-blowing site.

● **RIGHT OFF I-40,** Meteor Crater is located around 64km (40 miles) east of Flagstaff and 27km (17 miles) from Winslow.

CALIFORNIA, USA

RACETRACK PLAYA

As my 4WD slammed over the ruts of Racetrack Rd in Death Valley National Park, I tried to keep my bones from rattling right out of my body. With miles of washboard ahead and empty desert all around, I felt vulnerable and alone. But then again, that was the point.

My goal? Observing the mysterious moving rocks of the Racetrack Playa, a dry lakebed in the park's northern wilds. I was living in LA at the time, trying to break in as a screenwriter. But success was elusive. As a goal-oriented person, I decided to tackle a series of challenging outdoor adventures: mini-successes would keep me fired up.

But then I met Racetrack Valley Rd. A 32km (20 mile) unpaved nightmare in a desert valley flanked by dark mountains. How nightmarish? The park recommends a 4WD. A spare tyre is also smart. Mobile-phone coverage? Nope. Plus, Charles Manson and his followers holed up in Death Valley's southern reaches after the Helter Skelter murders; misfits and malcontents were no strangers here.

Teakettle Junction finally appeared; the playa was 10km (6 miles) ahead. Anticipation overtook fear, and at the parking area I left the car and approached the lakebed. Boulders dotted the parched earth before me. In their wake, trails were carved into the dirt. How did the rocks move? Some weighed more than 300kg (661lb). That question had vexed observers for decades. Aliens? Supernatural forces? Scientists solved the mystery in 2013. In winter, a thin ice sheet occasionally covers the playa. As the ice warms, it cracks apart. Winds push these ice patches into rocks that have tumbled from surrounding mountains, and these wind-driven floes shove the rocks across the slick lakebed. After temperatures rise, the ice vaporises, leaving the boulders and their tracks.

I walked, took pictures. Mesmerising. But I had a long journey back, so I didn't linger. My return? Bumpy, but fun. I'd accomplished my goal. Even better – I'd seen something rare, which triggered a sense of lightness and wonder. Maybe there was magic left in the world. The mystery has been solved, but the stark beauty of the setting and the rarity of the phenomenon keep this place amazing. *–AMY BALFOUR*

THE BOULDERS DOT the southern end of the playa. Reach the Racetrack by driving down Racetrack Valley Rd. Driving across the playa or anywhere off established roads is prohibited. Don't walk across the playa when it is wet. The western border of the park is 370km (230 miles) from Los Angeles.

PINEAPPLE GARDEN MAZE

Covering over 12,000 sq metres (130,000 sq ft), the Pineapple Garden Maze is the biggest permanent hedge maze in the Americas. Designated the world's largest such maze by Guinness World Records in 2008 (but since overtaken by China's Yancheng Dafeng Dream Maze), it's the signature attraction at O'ahu's Dole Pineapple Plantation. Wander a labyrinth of Hawaiian croton, hibiscus, panax and pineapple and see if you can beat the fastest times through the maze – winners receive prizes for finding eight 'secret stations' hidden within the structure's plant-formed walls. The fastest times recorded were around seven minutes, but the average wanderer takes about an hour to complete the maze. It's at its best just after a heavy rain, when the plants are at their most colourful.

● **THE DOLE PLANTATION** is on Kamehameha Hwy, about 40 minutes from Waikīkī.

FÉIS AN EILEIN

Féis An Eilein translates as 'island festival' – and the use of Gaelic is central to what this community event is all about. Held in the gloriously rural Cape Breton village of Christmas Island, this week of voice, music and dance celebrates all things Celtic. There are storytelling sessions and song workshops, concerts and ceilidhs, walks and many chances to hear fiddlers work their musical magic. And if you've never been to a traditional Milling Frolic, now's your chance. With a view to preserving the language and culture of the region's Scottish forebears, Gaelic is spoken and sung throughout the week.

It's one of three Christmas Islands in the world, and local legend accords that this one is named after a local Mi'kmaq tribal chief, who had strong connections with French settlers and took the name Noel.

● **FÉIS AN EILEIN** is held annually in August. Fly to Sydney in Nova Scotia and hire a car for the 60km (37 mile) drive to Christmas Island.

CULEBRA, PUERTO RICO

PLAYA FLAMENCO TANKS

Playa Flamenco, located on the Puerto Rican island of Culebra, is often lauded as the country's premier spot to soak up some sun, but this pearly little stretch of paradise wasn't always a laid-back place to relax. In the 1930s, the US Navy claimed all of Culebra's public lands and began using them for bombing practice and military exercises – activity that only intensified during the Vietnam War in the 1960s. In 1971, Culebra locals began protesting the US naval presence on the island, and their efforts eventually led to the discontinuation of military exercises there. Today, remnants of this era are still present – two rusting US tanks sink into the soft sands of Playa Flamenco. Puerto Ricans have covered one of them with art and graffiti, turning a solemn reminder of occupation into a brightly coloured symbol of civil resistance.

● **GET TO CULEBRA** from Puerto Rico's mainland on the ferry from Fajardo. It's a 30-minute walk to the beach from Dewey.

GEORGIA, USA

OLD CAR CITY

Cadillac Ranch in Texas isn't the only rural automobile installation worth visiting in the car-crazy USA. Old Car City in White, Georgia, is a fascinating mashup of open-air classic-car museum and nature preserve. Spend an afternoon walking the 10km (6 miles) of nature trails as they wind through one of the most beautiful junkyards in the world, filled with more than 4000 complete cars from no later than 1972. The forest has reclaimed many of the vehicles, creating an ethereal, postapocalyptic atmosphere.

Run by Dean Lewis as a labour of love, the 14-hectare (35-acre) lot was originally purchased by his parents in 1931 as a site for a general store. They started a car dealership here as well, and Lewis has kept up this tradition for decades.

● **OLD CAR CITY,** an hour's drive from Atlanta, opens Tuesday to Saturday, 9am to 4pm.

LA CASA DE PASCUALITA

Long before people fell in love with AI chatbots, nonhumans have tugged at the heartstrings of the living. La Pascualita, a Mexican mannequin dressed in bridal splendour, has enjoyed an especially unusual romantic life. She spent decades gazing seductively from the window of a bridal clothing boutique in Chihuahua, causing a French magician to become so obsessed that he would visit the shop window every night. She's even rumoured to come alive at night to dance.

Local fixations on La Pascualita can be explained by her resemblance to the former shop-owner's daughter, who is said to have died of a spider bite on her wedding day in 1930. Frozen in time before she could utter "till death do us part," it's no wonder she has become a romantic icon for local brides.

From the clefts in her hands to her lush eyelashes, La Pascualita looks uncannily human, leading to whispers that she is an embalmed body rather than a shop dummy. It isn't physically possible for a corpse to remain so beautiful for so many years (we checked). But when faced with La Pascualita, looking into her dewy brown eyes and noticing the quiver of trepidation on her mulberry-stained lips, you might feel a flicker of doubt. That is, if you're lucky enough to see her.

Recently, locals say La Pascualita is seldom displayed at the bridal store these days (corner of Calle Guadalupe Victoria and Av Melchor Ocampo); there's an alternative doll horror show at Mexico City's Isla de las Muñecas.

● **AT THE TIME** of writing, travel was not advised to the state of Chihuahua in Mexico.

LA SOUFRIÈRE VOLCANO

In 1995, life changed forever for residents of the small island of Montserrat, a British Overseas Territory in the southeastern Caribbean. On 18 July, the Soufrière Volcano erupted, sending massive pyroclastic flows across the south of the island and burying most of the capital, Plymouth, as well as the surrounding towns and forests. The eruptions left two-thirds of Montserrat covered in volcanic sludge and ash, permanently altering the landscape. The volcano awoke again in 1997, destroying the airport. The affected areas were among the island's most populated, and in the years after the eruptions the population shrank significantly; it now stands at around 4500 people.

Today, the region resembles a modern Pompeii, the sloping grey face extending into the deep blue of the Caribbean Sea. Plymouth stands as a city immobilised, with rooftops and church steeples peeking out from the solidified ash, ghosts of a busy urban life that once existed in the heart of Caribbean paradise. However, in these tangible reminders of the devastation, Montserrat is finding the silver lining – the volcano zone has become the island's biggest tourist attraction. Visitors can see the volcanic aftermath from a number of viewpoints, or visit the Montserrat Volcano Observatory to learn more about the 1995 eruption as well as the still-active volcano's most recent rumblings.

● **ACCESS MONTSERRAT FROM** Antigua via puddle-jumper flights with Fly Montserrat or BMN SVG Airways.

UNSETTLING HOTELS

Hotels are a refuge where travellers can kick off their shoes and exhale the tensions of the day. But they can also be the opposite: disconcerting places where privacy is an illusion and dreams of the past disturb your sleep. Tinker with the emotional temperature of your next trip by staying in one of these disquieting hotels.

TALLINN, ESTONIA

1. HOTEL VIRU

Surveillance was rife in Soviet-era Tallinn, and foreign visitors weren't funnelled into the Viru for its views: each of its 60 rooms was bugged. Today, there's a KGB Museum in the former surveillance room, brimming with 1970s radio equipment and gas masks, and the rooms are free of hidden microphones.

PYONGYANG, NORTH KOREA

2. RYUGYONG HOTEL

Don't try to stay at this 105-storey hotel in the world's most secretive country. Rumours are rife about why this vast triangle is unfinished after 30 years of construction and $750 million invested.

SIIN EI OLE MIDAGI
ЗДЕСЬ НИЧЕГО НЕТ

変なホテル
Henn na Hotel

UNSETTLING HOTELS

LIEPĀJA, LATVIA

3. KAROSTA PRISON

Test your nerves at Liepāja's century-old ex-military prison, complete with bullying staff and a rusty door slamming shut. Warning: the Nazi and Soviet prisoners once locked in these cells may trouble your dreams.

COLORADO, USA

4. THE STANLEY HOTEL

This 1909 hotel, near Rocky Mountains National Park, inspired Stephen King to write *The Shining*. It's also the location of repeated sightings of long-dead previous owners.

PORTSMOUTH, ENGLAND

5. NO MAN'S FORT

The threat of attacks by Napoleon III stirred the British to fortify their sea defences and build No Man's Fort. Temporarily reincarnated as a luxury hotel, it's now under new ownership – stay tuned for future fortress stays.

MONMOUTHSHIRE, WALES

6. DECOY BUNKER

British defence forces lit fires here in WWII to fox German bombers into thinking the twinkling light was an all-important munitions factory. The domed roof is no longer a place to duck for cover – in fact, you're likely to get a snug night's sleep.

MASSACHUSETTS, USA

7. LIZZIE BORDEN HOUSE

Immortalised in a grisly nursery rhyme, this 19th-century Fall River guesthouse is the place where Lizzie allegedly dealt out 40 whacks with an axe. Book a ghost tour while you're here. If you survive, you're in the right spot for more spooky sights; witchy Salem is just 1½ hours' drive away.

TOKYO, JAPAN

8. HENN NA HOTEL

This hotel chain is either unsettling or efficient, depending on your feelings about robot receptionists and facial recognition. The Maihama Tokyo Bay property offers a robotic dinosaur welcome.

CALIFORNIA, USA

9. CECIL HOTEL

Inspiring TV's *American Horror Story*, the Cecil was the site of three murders and many suicides, a former residence of serial killer Richard Ramirez, and where student Elisa Lam met her unexplained death in 2013. After a failed rebranding, this Los Angeles hotel became an affordable housing complex in 2021.

FLORENCE, ITALY

10. HOTEL BURCHIANTI

Even guests who are sceptics at check-in emerge the next morning with tales of ghostly maids and poltergeist groping. At least sleepless nights allow time to admire the ceiling frescoes and four-posters.

HAVANA, CUBA

FUSTERLANDIA

Havana's most remarkable work of art isn't a sculpture or a painting, but a whole neighbourhood. Fusterlandia is the unofficial name for Jaimanitas, a quiet suburb that's best known for its giddy array of mosaics, murals and whimsical Gaudí-esque works by Cuban artist José Fuster.

Fuster's project began as a spot of home decoration in the mid-1990s, but morphed into something more ambitious. By the 2010s, his decorative ceramics and paintings had covered several blocks, encompassing street signs, public spaces and more than 80 houses. Doused in bright Caribbean sunshine, the intricate tile work, curvaceous parapets and kaleidoscope of colours create a spectacle that makes Barcelona's Park Güell look positively sedate.

Welcoming you to the 'show' is the Jaimanitas neighbourhood sign, etched with words 'Homenaje a Gaudí' (Homage to Gaudí) in vivid mosaic. The father of Spanish Modernisme isn't Fuster's only influence; a nearby public bench in front of a wave-shaped wall is covered in tiles painted with Picasso-like visages. Yet Fusterlandia is inherently Cuban. A block away, a huge mural depicts the 1956 landing of the *Granma* yacht, with Fidel Castro, Che Guevara and Camilo Cienfuegos on board. Equally head-swivelling are reproductions of the Cuban flag, surreal studies of the Virgin of Charity (Cuba's patron saint), and a terrace of houses (Fuster's neighbours) with a different letter of 'Viva Cuba' on each chimney.

The district's benches, bus stops and even a doctor's surgery all get the Fuster treatment; next to the artist's home, a chess park contains a life-sized board with *Alice in Wonderland*-like kings, queens and knights. But Fusterlandia's pièce de résistance is the artist's home: a maelstrom of murals, arches, lurid faces and swirling ceramic trees and flowers. The multilevelled complex is centred around a pool, replete with mythical maritime themes (recalling Jaimanitas' fishing background) and enlivened with mermaids, fisherfolk and a giant octopus.

For a bird's-eye view, climb to a small observation deck to absorb the fantasy, exuberance and, above all, overriding sunniness. Fuster's house is also home to his taller (workshop), where it's possible to acquire a piece of the master's art or, if you're lucky, watch him at work. –*BRENDAN SAINSBURY*

JAIMANITAS LIES 20KM (12 MILES) west of central Havana. Bus P4 stops nearby, or you can take a taxi. Entrance to Fuster's house is free. Make sure to review current travel advisories before planning a trip.

GROTTO OF THE BLESSED VIRGIN MARY

Motoring past the tidy green lawns in Munster, Indiana – a working-class community near Chicago – you barely notice the low-slung buildings of Our Lady of Mount Carmel Monastery behind a thicket of trees. But the Discalced Carmelite Fathers have been tending their trippy, fluorescent rock grotto here for more than 60 years.

The barefoot monks, as they're known, arrived from Poland after WWII. One of the friars was also a geologist, so when they decided to build a one-of-a-kind shrine to the Virgin Mary in 1954, this guy knew just what to do. First came 230 tonnes (254 tons) of sponge rock for the grotto's dark, twisting, three-storey caverns. Then came the bright-hued bits of rose quartz, blue fluorite and other minerals that glimmer in starry designs from the walls. The real showstopper, though, is the Fluorescent Altar. Flip the light switch and the stones around Mary's statue jolt to life. You don't see the message at first, but then the rocks start to glow yellow and green – and 'Hail Holy Queen' appears in all its psychedelic glory.

More ultraviolet goodness radiates in the nearby Memorial Chapel, where there's a shrine to Jesus raising the dead. The monks show the sun dropping, hands clawing from the earth, yellow crosses marching across the ceiling – conveyed entirely with glow-in-the-dark rocks. Even Michelangelo would rub his eyes in wonder.

● **THE MONASTERY IS** open on Sundays, from April through to October, or by appointment. You'll need a car, as it's a 50km (31 mile) drive from downtown Chicago.

ANIAKCHAK NATIONAL MONUMENT

More people explore space each year than visit Aniakchak, a collapsed volcanic crater that contains some of the rawest wilderness in North America. Fresh off the angry Bering Sea, waterfalls of billowing clouds spill over the steep crater rim during wet weather, adding a ghostly sheen to the 'lost world' of giant bears and barren tundra below. Adventurous types can backpack into the crater along sinuous animal trails, before whitewater-rafting out along foamy Aniakchak River to the sea – you'll need foldable kayaks, lightweight camping equipment and lots of courage.

● **FLY INTO THE** tiny settlement of Port Heiden and hike from there.

HIDDEN BEACH

The Marietas' secret beaches are a sought-after sight, but so-called Hidden Beach is the cherry on top. Sliding off the side of a catamaran, I swim with the tide until I reach a thin slit – like the lip of a closed clamshell – between the surface of the sea and the arid island above. I duck under the waves, quickly resurfacing in a rocky chasm that leads towards the doughnut hole at the island's core, ringed by a spit of peachy sand. Archaeologists and volcanologists have posited theories of the beach's strange shape based on evidence of ancient deity worship and modern-day bomb testing – today it's an anomaly dutifully captured on social media by its visitors. *–BRANDON PRESSER*

● **A SHORT BOAT** ride connects the Marietas to Riviera Nayarit, serviced by the international airport in Puerto Vallarta. Make sure to review current travel advisories before planning a trip.

APOSTLE ISLANDS SEA CAVES

Nature is the artist at the Apostle Islands National Lakeshore. Waves slicing across Lake Superior have transformed this honey-coloured archipelago into a monumental display: leaning towers of sandstone, natural archways that frame the turquoise water, and formidable rock formations that resemble Futurist sculptures.

At 82,103 sq km (31,700 sq miles), Lake Superior has the largest area of any freshwater lake in the world. This made it easy to misname its sinuous caverns as sea caves. Layer by golden layer, the sandstone stacks took a million years to form; some of the most spectacular are at Devils Island. Guided tours lead kayakers to paddle under ochre archways and listen to the echo of water sloshing inside the caves. (Three-hour cruises on larger boats are an exertion-free alternative.)

Summer gives the islands a burnished glow, and under cloud cover you'll notice bluish minerals glinting out from the rock. During storms, the surging waves thunder into the caves and kick up spectacular spray. But winter can bring the greatest masterpiece: when freezing temperatures combine with lashing winds that stir the waves, the splashing of frigid water creates ice caves, complete with frosty stalactites that resemble white fangs. Tragically, rising temperatures resulting from climate change are making this phenomenon vanishingly rare; the last winter with stable ice caves was 2015.

* **JUNE TO OCTOBER** is prime time for getting out on the water with a pair of oars. Base yourself in Bayfield (less than 150km/93 miles from Duluth Airport). In winter, check the National Parks Service website for updates on the ice caves (fingers crossed...).

RAINBOW EUCALYPTUS TREES

The serpentine 'Road to Hana' is one of the most incredible drives anywhere on the planet, featuring an overwhelming abundance of sights, sounds and colours, as the tarmac winds its way down to the sleepy town nestled in the fragrant bosom of Maui's rainforest. An oft-overlooked sight that you can see on this journey is the 'painted forest' of rainbow eucalyptus trees, right at the roadside: a quirk of nature producing trees that literally look like frozen rainbows. The reds, purples and greens are particularly vivid within these spectacular oddities of evolution, thanks to sections of bark shedding at different times during the year. However, the real beauty of this phenomenon is that the process is ongoing: the multicoloured streaks continuously evolve, forming a grove of living kaleidoscopes.

THE RAINBOW EUCALYPTUS grove can be found at mile marker 7 on Maui's Hana Hwy (park carefully). You can also see some of the trees at the nearby Ke'anae Arboretum.

IGLESIA DE SAN JUAN BAUTISTA

Maya rituals fuse with Catholic worship at this high-altitude village in the Chiapas. As you step through the church's ornate green entrance archway, you're enveloped by the scent of incense, candle smoke and pine needles, which are strewn across the floor. The faithful mutter fervent prayers in the Tzotzil language and employ bones, eggs, Coca-Cola and sugarcane liqueur in curative and protective rituals. Locals are fiercely protective of these unique rites; make sure you heed the 'no pictures' rule inside the church. Outsiders may be invited to participate in rituals outside the church, for a fee.

* **AT THE TIME** of writing, travel was not advised to the state of Chiapas.

LOUISIANA, USA

NICOLAS CAGE'S TOMB

Dark-hearted travellers have many reasons to cemetery-hop in New Orleans, like sighing over Gothic statues and paying homage at a voodoo priestess' grave. But some tombs still wait to be filled – like the grave of still-living actor Nicolas Cage, notorious for his meme-worthy facial expressions and inexhaustible method acting. Cage's past purchases include European castles and a rare Mongolian dinosaur skull, so a 2.7m/8.9ft-tall pyramid tomb in St Louis Cemetery No 1 seems entirely on brand. Note the mysterious inscription on the dazzling white cone: *Omnia ab Uno* (Everything from One).

* **GUIDED TOURS LEAD** visitors through St Louis Cemetery No 1, showing off a motley crew of the venerably interred.

BRITISH COLUMBIA, CANADA

WHISTLER TRAIN WRECK SITE

My husband and I are hiking near Whistler in British Columbia, hunting for a rather unique view: a wrecked train that's become an outdoor art canvas.

In 1956, a freight train travelling too fast through a rock canyon derailed near this Canadian mountain community, 120km (75 miles) north of Vancouver. To clear the rail line, a logging company towed the damaged train cars into the woods, where they were abandoned. Eventually, local graffiti artists found the wreckage in the old-growth forest and started using the derelict railcars as a canvas.

For years, the only way to reach the site was to hike along an active rail line – not the safest choice. This all changed with the construction of a suspension bridge over the Cheakamus River, which made this unexpected artistic hub much easier to reach... as long as you don't miss the turnoff for the path.

Retracing our steps, we find an entry to the Sea to Sky Trail, a long-distance hiking route that extends through Whistler into the BC wilderness. We follow the trail into the woods and soon spot a sign, 'Train Wreck Site and Suspension Bridge'. The path takes us down to the churning river and over the wooden bridge that sways gently as we cross. And suddenly, in the middle of the forest, we're in a street-art gallery. Seven mangled railcars sit at weird angles in a sun-dappled grove, each tagged and retagged with vividly coloured paint. Cartoonish portraits, wildlife murals and indecipherable scrawls overlap on this ever-changing canvas, and it's not just graffiti artists who have customised the train-wreck site. Mountain bikers have built jumps and rails surrounding several of the train cars, creating a renegade bike playground.

We snap plenty of photos before making our way back over the bridge and through the woods. Just a short distance from North America's largest winter-sports resort, it feels as if we've discovered a secret art gallery. It's not secret, of course – but you do have to know where to look. *– CAROLYN B HELLER*

SOUTH OF WHISTLER, the train wreck is a 30-minute walk along the Sea to Sky Trail, which you can pick up behind the Hi Whistler Hostel.

OLE-BOLLE
HUS

PACIFIC NORTHWEST TROLL HUNTING

WASHINGTON & OREGON

There's no need to peer under bridges to find Thomas Dambo's trolls – the Danish artist has resurrected these moody monsters from Nordic folklore and let them loose in locations around the world. Fashioned from reclaimed wood by Dambo and his army of volunteers, each troll has a distinct personality – but they all feel right at home in the temperate rainforests of Washington state and Oregon. Here in the Pacific Northwest, Dambo's trolls lurk in cool glades and parks, and even sometimes loiter in cities.

"A lot of the locations where you'll find my work are old airstrips, landfill that's been turned into a park, or a piece of forest that has been abandoned," explains Dambo. "My trolls don't like to live where humans are close by."

Despite their attempts to flee human company, the trolls have become a cult attraction, and you can meet a few on this road trip around Seattle and Portland.

TO CATCH 'EM all in a single trip, you'll need your own wheels. You can also troll-hunt by public transport. In Seattle, buses 554 and 40 run from downtown to Issaquah and Ballard, and from the ferry terminal to Vashon and Bainbridge Islands. In Portland, bus 45 runs to Ole Bolle.

PACIFIC NORTHWEST TROLL HUNTING

JAKOB TWO TREES, *ISSAQUAH, WASHINGTON*

A wooden troll towers 4m (13ft) high in a forest glade south of old-town Issaquah, 25km (16 miles) east of Seattle. But despite his mighty stature, he looks nervous. "My trolls are scared of humans because they're the enemy to the natural world," declares Dambo. "We are the invasive species that's destroying the whole planet."

FRANKIE FEETSPLINTER, *BALLARD, WASHINGTON*

Standing with a toothy grin, Frankie isn't a typical troll skulking in the shadows – he's more like an oversized museum usher, keeping watch outside the National Nordic Museum in Ballard, 10km (6 miles) north of Seattle. Like all of Dambo's trolls, he's built from recycled wood – often used wooden pallets – and thousands of screws.

As a self-styled 'recycle artist', Dambo is resolute about making his art from materials that are discarded or underloved. "Our minds are so creative that we can build anything," explains Dambo. "You can make something that is super beautiful and special from what is just around you. Our trash is a treasure."

OSCAR THE BIRD KING, *VASHON ISLAND, WASHINGTON*

Not all of Dambo's trolls will look pleased to see you. Throne-seated Oscar is one of the most imposing of Dambo's sculptures. Seated regally in Point Robinson Park on Vashon Island, he has a beard of branches, a crown of birdhouses and points an accusing finger. This troll isn't afraid of humans' impact on the natural world – he's calling us out on it.

PIA THE PEACEKEEPER, *BAINBRIDGE ISLAND, WASHINGTON*

Sitting cross-legged beneath the alder and Pacific madrone trees in Sakai Park, 5.5m/18ft-tall Pia exudes thoughtfulness. She's a perfect reflection of Bainbridge Island's peaceful atmosphere; its charming gardens, parks and public art inspire many Seattleites to wonder if they should quit the city hustle.

The trolls reflect the values of the community that brought them to life; in Pia's case, her creators were scout and cub troops, park services and Dambo's own team. "I'll design components of my sculptures in order to allow a lot of people to participate," explains Dambo. "I see my whole project as showcasing the value of our leftovers – all the resources that we discard."

OLE BOLLE TROLL, *PORTLAND, OREGON*

Dambo's trolls have even roamed as far as 265km (165 miles) south, to the Nordic Northwest campus in Portland. Here, Ole Bolle kneels over a human-sized wooden cabin and peers in through the skylight. Step inside the cabin to see him looking down at you. "It's like when we humans look into a pet hamster cage or a birdhouse," enthuses Dambo. "You become the little one."

PREVIOUS PAGE: Ole Bolle Troll peeping into a cabin in Portland

THIS PAGE: Forest-dwelling troll Jakob sports a garland of birdhouses in Issaquah

NINE MILE CANYON

Tucked away in the fiery sandstone mountains of rugged Utah is one of the world's largest – and oldest – outdoor art galleries. Nine Mile Canyon (which is actually 74km/46 miles long, but was originally formed by Nine Mile Creek), contains thousands of ancient petroglyphs, carved by the native Fremont and Ute tribes between 600 and 1300 CE. The scenes – scattered throughout the canyon and easily accessible from the road running through it – depict everything from war and sacrifice to animal husbandry and family dynamics.

This spectacular visual storytelling is best explored with a local guide, who will help you peel away the respective layers (historically, not literally – there are signs everywhere reminding people not to touch the fragile rock art). A guide will also be able to point out petroglyphs, which you might otherwise have missed, as well as a number of (remarkably intact) ancient dwellings called pit houses. One way or another you'll need transport, but the canyon is a great day-trip option, with plenty of picturesque picnicking spots along the 160km (99 mile) round-trip from the town of Price. Visitors are advised to pack plenty of provisions for the journey (there are no shops or restaurants en route), as well as the free brochure detailing the canyon's main sites, which can be grabbed from the Carbon County Visitors Centre in Price.

* **NINE MILE CANYON** is accessible from Price, southeast on US Rte 6 then north on to Soldier Creek Rd.

VIRGINIA, USA

ASSATEAGUE ISLAND'S FERAL HORSES

Assateague, a barrier island off the coast of Virginia, is most famous for its herd of wild horses. There are numerous theories about how they first arrived here, ranging from them surviving a shipwreck off the Virginia coast to the more likely explanation that they were shipped in by canny mainland owners in order to avoid livestock taxes. These steeds are beautiful and fascinating to observe, forming bands of up to 12 that roam the island together. The horses can be viewed by visiting the Assateague Island National Seashore, which stretches across 60km (37 miles) of pristine coastline and is split by the borders of Maryland and Virginia. Be mindful that these are wild animals: don't feed them or get too close.

* **YOU'LL NEED YOUR** own wheels to get around the park; drive in from Ocean City (Maryland) or Chincoteague (Virginia). It's open all year-round.

DIQUÍS DELTA, COSTA RICA

DIQUÍS SPHERES

Scattered around the Diquís Delta on the west coast of Costa Rica are giant stone spheres – the only remnants of the mysterious Diquís civilisation that existed between 300 BCE and 1500 CE. Their purpose remains unknown, though theories suggest that those spheres found aligned in a certain way and may have functioned as solar calendars, while others were symbols of an individual's power (the bigger the sphere, the more powerful the chief).

You can see them in public parks in Palmar Sur and Sierpe, though the best place to view them is the Sitio Arqueológico Finca 6 museum, where the spheres have been left in their original alignments.

* **THE MUSEUM OPENS** 8am to 4pm, Tuesday to Sunday. Buses run between Sierpe and Palmar Sur.

WINCHESTER MYSTERY HOUSE

When media tycoon William Randolph Hearst hired architects to create the lavish and labyrinthine Hearst Castle on his California ranch, he was hailed as an eccentric genius with impeccable taste. When heiress Sarah Winchester oversaw her own opulent construction project, she was dubbed a grief-stricken madwoman plagued by ghosts.

Heir to the Winchester rifle fortune – 'the gun that won the West' – Sarah allegedly became interested in the occult after the deaths of her child and husband. According to local lore, Sarah sought comfort from a local medium following the untimely deaths of her child and husband. The medium told her the bad fortune was caused by spirits of those who had been killed by Winchester guns and wanted revenge, so Sarah spent the rest of her life trying to outwit these restless ghosts. But in 1880s America, it wasn't unknown for accomplished women like Sarah to be tarnished as unstable – especially those who held feminist-leaning beliefs.

Part of a family of architecture enthusiasts, Sarah was an avid attendee of design expos. After purchasing Llanada Villa in San Jose, California in 1886, she decided to direct its reconstruction herself. Now known as the Winchester Mystery House, the villa has over 160 rooms, 2000 doors and countless intriguing details: cabinets open to rooms, staircases go up then down, chimneys don't reach the roof. Sarah oversaw every detail, from carved wooden ceilings to imported European glass.

Many local legends emphasise Sarah's occultist practices and eccentricities, all of which are unproven. It's said that she always wore a veil over her face and fired staff (that she paid generously) if they saw her without it; that a bell tower chimed for lunch and dinner but also at midnight and 2am (the times of the departure and arrival of spirits); and that the house and its constant construction were a means of forming a labyrinth to keep her safe.

In fact, the property's quirks may be explained by circumstances. Sarah was small in stature, so short staircases have an unusually high number of steps. Doors to nowhere are the result of construction projects that had to be abandoned because of damage to the house in the 1906 earthquake.

It's impossible not to think of Sarah as you wander the home, and there have been ghostly sightings of people resembling Sarah and her employees. But don't expect an agonised spirit streaking down the halls – Sarah Winchester is more likely to glide calmly through the house, pondering the next detail of her architectural labour of love.

VISIT BY CAR or take the number 60 VTA bus from Santa Clara Station. There are guided tours daily.

SMOKING HILLS

Curls of white smoke rise like flags from Canada's Cape Bathurst. Within the rocky layers of the Smoking Hills (Ingniryuat), sulphur-rich brown coal auto-combusts when it's exposed to the air – a process that happens on repeat, as the action of the tides sloughs away hunks of the cliffs. This erosion elicits a near-constant billowing of hellish smoke, which carries its eggy odour of sulphur dioxide high into the air and stains the rocks a Plutonian colour palette, from maroon and orange to deathly grey.

More than once, this unearthly scene has been mistaken for signs of life. In the 1850s, explorer Robert McClure squinted out from his ship, the HMS *Investigator*, and thought elatedly that the smoke was a distress signal from John Franklin's lost expedition. In fact, these hissing hills have persisted for as many as 10,000 years, and they are likely to deceive passing sailors for centuries yet.

● **BETWEEN THE SINGEING** heat and noxious fumes, it isn't safe to come anywhere close to the Smoking Hills. Some cruises, like those run by Adventure Life, ply the Northwest Passage and get near enough for your zoom lens.

UNCLAIMED BAGGAGE CENTER

This Scottsboro oddity delivers the goods in more ways than one. Part jumbo-sized thrift store, part museum of an extraordinary range of misplaced items, this labyrinth of lost goods is awe-inspiring in scale and an excellent place to pick up some cheap cowboy boots.

If you've ever wondered what happens to luggage that loses its way and never quite gets reunited with its owner, it could well be at the Unclaimed Baggage Center. What waits within the store are racks of (laundered) clothing and piles of electronic devices, plus enough quirky items to happily pass half a day. Staff also run insightful demonstrations of the art of unpacking someone else's lost bag and deciding what gets to go on sale here.

● **THE UNCLAIMED BAGGAGE** Center is two hours' drive from Nashville and opens Monday to Saturday.

ACTUN TUNICHIL MUKNAL

The cave was black. My weak headlamp lit only as far as my next step. But when our guide Juan Carlos shined his powerful light, the space opened up into a vast cavern. So this is what the underworld looks like, I thought. We had journeyed deep into Actun Tunichil Muknal, following in the footsteps of the ancient Maya who frequented this cave network, seeking a route to the underworld and a way to communicate with its gods. Our group had come to see what they'd left.

THE CAVES ARE in the Cayo district of Belize, and are accessible only on licensed tours.

After an hour, we gathered on a dry ledge. "You will walk where I walk and stand where I tell you to," Juan Carlos instructed. "There are artefacts everywhere." He shone his light on the ground, where a broken pot was one of many strewn around the chamber. He explained that they were used for food offerings and blood-letting rituals in which a Maya ruler would mix blood with incense and burn it as an offering.

After potholing through the cave and seeing these ancient artefacts, it was hard to imagine what might come next. But then, Juan Carlos' torch illuminated a 1500-year-old skull; other bones were scattered nearby, all belonging to a 40-year-old male. He was the first of many skeletons that we saw in Actun Tunichil Muknal, which contains the remains of 14 individuals – all victims of human sacrifice – including a complete skeleton of a young woman, encrusted in calcium carbonate and sparkling in our torch beams. Juan Carlos set a scene for us: "Imagine this room lit with torches," he said, as his light cast shadows on the walls. "Imagine the air is filled with chanting." Then, referring to the hallucinogenic morning glory flowers we'd seen outside: "Now imagine that you are high. No wonder the Maya believed that they were communicating with gods." No wonder, indeed. –*MARA VORHEES*

THE VILLAGE OF CHICKEN

I wanted wilderness. I wanted adventure. I wanted to drive the open road. Heading through Alaska on the Top of the World Highway, a summer-only mountain byway, seemed like the ideal plan. Until I arrived in Chicken.

A handful of log cabins in the middle of nowhere, Chicken is a tiny speck in a landscape that is colossal, unforgiving and raw. And, oh, it has a bar with a cannon that shoots underwear into the air; its saloon festooned with knickers, baseball hats, licence plates and handwritten notes. Chicken is one of Alaska's last gold-rush remnants – when the highway closes in October, the population drops to single figures and the village succumbs to isolation and the Arctic winter. In summer a trickle of prospectors, intrepid 4WD drivers and thrill-seekers visit to try their luck in the creeks, to learn about frontier history or tick off one more kooky adventure.

Early prospectors arrived here in the late 1800s and only survived their first winter thanks to the abundance of ptarmigan (a type of wild grouse). By 1902, the tent city needed a name. The miners wanted to call it after the local bird but no one could agree on the spelling, so they opted for Chicken. The giftshop is full of 'I got laid in Chicken' mugs and 'Cluck it' T-shirts, the creeks still spit out gleaming nuggets, and you can tour a working mine or pan for gold (you can also cheat via a hired metal detector or a bag of giftshop gold flakes).

It's a weird and wonderful place, populated by oddballs and eccentrics, and ideal for kayaking down isolated rivers where your only company are moose and bears. That is, if you don't arrive during Chickenstock, the annual music festival, when almost 1000 revellers descend on the village to listen to folk and bluegrass and, yes, do the chicken dance. With music blaring, merry punters stumbling to the public outhouse under the midnight sun, and knickers blasting from a cannon, there's a strong whiff of the old Wild West. Anything goes when you're this far from civilisation.

–ETAIN O'CARROLL

THERE'S NO PUBLIC transport and the highway closes from October to April. You could fly from Tok, but that's cheating.

Chicken Alaska
Yok Spring 47
Rooster Door
Cluck NM
Barnyard KY
Chickaboogalla Australia miles
Lizard Lick NC
Suck Egg Hollow TN miles
Roosterberg Belgium 4305 miles
Lizzard KY

BRITISH COLUMBIA, CANADA

THE FELLED GOLDEN SPRUCE

There once stood a Sitka spruce unlike any other. Its boughs were bright yellow rather than deep green, and it stood out against the old-growth rainforest of Haida Gwaii as though sunlight poured from its very branches. The strange colour was the result of a rare genetic mutation that caused the tree to lack the chlorophyll normally found in spruces. Against a backdrop of green, the 50m (164ft) golden spruce was an unusual sight.

The tree was a popular stop on visitors' itineraries, and central to legends of the Indigenous people, the Haida, who named it K'iid K'iyass (Old Tree). That is until 1997 when, after standing for over 300 years, the 2m/7ft-thick tree was cut down by an environmental activist called Grant Hadwin in protest against the destruction of nearby forests.

But the golden spruce lives on. Cuttings taken from the original tree were distributed across British Columbia. At Millennium Park in Port Clements, some 10km (6 miles) north of where the golden spruce fell, an offspring grows behind a barbed-wire fence – at around 1m (3.3ft) tall, it's a mere echo of the original. Just outside town, the Golden Spruce Trail takes hikers to the edge of the Yakoun River, where the tree could once be seen. Now the decaying stump of the golden spruce rests on the riverbank.

HWY 16 CONNECTS Port Clements to the main Haida Gwaii transport hub of Skidegate Landing. Take Bayview St out of town, heading southbound for 6km (4 miles); the Golden Spruce Trailhead will be on your right.

SOUTH DAKOTA, USA

MONUMENT OF HUGH GLASS

When a furious mother bear mauls Leonardo DiCaprio in blockbuster movie *The Revenant*, his return from the brink of death seems like Hollywood fantasy – and yet it's based on real-life frontiersman Hugh Glass. He set out on a fur-trading expedition in 1823, but was attacked by a grizzly near the border of present-day North and South Dakota. Bleeding and unconscious, Glass was not expected to survive. His companions, unable to carry him to safety, buried him in a shallow grave and left him behind.

Glass survived. Driven by revenge but unable to walk, Glass crawled 320km (199 miles) to Fort Kiowa. However, the true story lacks a climactic ending: accounts differ on whether Glass had a change of heart, or simply never had a chance to enact his vengeful plan. He was killed by Native Americans in 1833.

* **A MARKER STANDS** in Shadehill, South Dakota, near the place Glass was mauled. Nearby Lemmon has a statue.

NEW MEXICO, USA

BISTI/DE-NA-ZIN WILDERNESS

There's a dreamscape of mushroom-cap towers and psychedelic sandstone in northwest New Mexico. Around 182 sq km (70 sq miles) of ravines, rocks and deep gullies make up the Bisti/De-Na-Zin Wilderness (from the Navajo words 'Dééł Náázíní' or 'standing cranes' – their sacred forms have been scratched into the stone at numerous sites). One of the world's most fossil-rich sedimentary basins, this land shelters petrified logs, insect fossils and colossal finds such as the 'Bisti Beast', an adult T-rex discovered in 1998. The most distinctive formations here are hoodoos, top-heavy rock chimneys chiselled away by the uneven forces of erosion – but Bisti/De-Na-Zin is a patchwork quilt of geological marvels. There are fanlike designs from ancient flood plains; maroon and white sandstone blurring together like Impressionist paintings; and egg-like boulders that wouldn't look out of place among the protuberant towers of Gaudí's Casa Batlló. Wander here long enough and you'll surely dream up a surrealist masterpiece.

* **FARMINGTON IS AN** ideal jumping-off point; there are two main access points to the wilderness, respectively 65km (40 miles) and 70km (43 miles) south of the city.

MONO LAKE TUFA STATE NATURAL RESERVE

Million-year-old Mono Lake looks its age, and we mean that as a compliment: it's surrounded by limestone spindles, known as tufa towers, which resemble long, wrinkled fingers. They sprout wherever freshwater springs well up from the bottom of the lake into its alkaline waters; the resulting chemical reaction creates solid calcium carbonate that builds up into cadaverous shapes.

It takes decades for the tufa towers to swell and grow, but they eventually break through the lake's surface and emerge like zombies. From a distance, your eyes play tricks: the towers look like a crowd of humanoid silhouettes hunched together in and around the water. On blue-sky days, Mono transforms into a mirror, instantly doubling its population of calcium carbonate gremlins; towards dusk, California's peachy light gives them an unearthly glow.

The lake's unusually high salinity has allowed it to build this petrified army. Doughnut-shaped and wrapped around the volcanic Paoha Island (the result of an eruption some 350 years ago), it has no tributaries flowing from it – giving the salty water nowhere else to go. Scientists estimate that 280 million tonnes (275 million tons) of salts are dissolved in just 3.66 sq km (1.4 sq miles) of water. But Mono Lake's pH is home sweet home for its trillions of brine shrimp – and for migratory birds, this excessively salty bisque is hard to resist.

● **MONO LAKE IS** easy to visit from the vastly more popular Lake Tahoe, which straddles the California–Nevada state border 160km (99 miles) north. Fly-and-drive from the international airports in San Francisco, Los Angeles or Las Vegas.

TREMENDOUS TOILETS

'In this world, nothing is certain except death and taxes' – so wrote Benjamin Franklin, who presumably scratched 'time on the toilet' from his first draft. Humankind's most universal activity has lingering taboos, but these can inspire bold architects and creators to elevate the humble commode. From inventive conveniences to a lavatorial artwork or a toilet-themed fun park, these wonderful water closets lend a certain grandeur to nature's call…

SUWON, SOUTH KOREA

1. MR TOILET HOUSE

Suppress your bashfulness at these monuments to the call of nature. From loos with views to sculptures that flush, Suwon's quirky theme park turns humanity's most basic necessity into a family day out, with attractions that edify the humble toilet in all its forms. Browse the toilet-shaped museum and snap photos of a big golden turd.

WELLINGTON, NEW ZEALAND

2. KUMUTOTO PUBLIC TOILETS

Affectionately dubbed the 'lobster loos', these concrete conveniences on Wellington's waterfront resemble a crustacean's lopped-off legs. Local architect Bret Thurston dreamed up the design, complete with updraft ventilation and red-steel armour to protect them from the oft-drizzly weather.

TREMENDOUS TOILETS

CALIFORNIA, USA

3. MADONNA INN

From cherry-coloured leather seats to rosy cocktails, no corner of San Luis Obispo's Madonna Inn is spared from indulgently pink design. But the toilets steal the show: there's a shimmering boudoir-style powder room for women and a waterfall urinal for gents... go with the flow!

SELÇUK, TÜRKIYE

4. EPHESUS TOILETS

There are no secrets in ancient bathhouses. The 1st-century-CE municipal loos at Ephesus archaeological site are a familiar sight, ovoid in shape and made of marble – except there are 36 of them laid out in long, sociable rows.

KITAKYUSHU, JAPAN

5. TOTO MUSEUM

The high-tech toilets of Japan, with waterjets, music and heated seats, are admired (and chuckled at) worldwide. Take the plunge and learn about their development at this museum of plumbing.

LONDON, ENGLAND

6. CELLARDOOR

Not keen on lingering all night in a lavatory? CellarDoor will change your mind. This basement public loo on Aldwych – once notorious in London's swinging scene –has been transformed into a chic cocktail bar.

MO, NORWAY

7. HULDEFOSSEN WATERFALL OUTHOUSE

Emerge from a simple wooden outhouse to the glorious sight of one of Norway's most admired waterfalls. Be assured that the sound of water tumbling from 92m (302ft) cliffs muffles any less pleasant sounds.

KAWAKAWA, NEW ZEALAND

8. HUNDERTWASSER TOILETS

Excuse yourself for a comfort break amid the undulating lines and vibrant colours of Austrian artist Friedensreich Hundertwasser – who lived for a quarter-century in this Bay of Islands town, and designed these lavish loos with bright mosaics and recycled stained glass.

AKASHI, JAPAN

9. HIPOPO PAPA CAFE

Answer the call of nature under the gaze of tropical fish at this cafe in Akashi. The women's bathroom is enclosed by a huge aquarium, so you can scrutinise a marine scene through floor-to-ceiling glass.

TENNESSEE, USA

10. ELVIS TOILET

The porcelain throne in the cordoned-off upper floor of Elvis' Memphis mansion is where the musical legend breathed (and strained) his last. Visitors to Graceland stand directly beneath the bathroom as they enter.

PARQUE FRANCISCO ALVARADO

If you're travelling through central Costa Rica, take a detour to Zarcero, a small town located in the western part of the Cordillera. There, you'll find Parque Francisco Alvarado, perhaps the country's most unusual public green space. Situated in front of the stately 17th-century Iglesia de San Rafael, the park started off as your average topiary garden. Then, in the 1960s, its gardener Evangelista Blanco Brenes decided to let his creativity flow, shaping the trees into dreamy, Dalí-esque forms. Today, the spot continues to function as an interactive botanical-art exhibit. Wind your way through a tunnel of 'melting' arches, or snap a photo with whimsical dancers, animals and dinosaurs.

★ **BUSES MAKE THE** drive to Zarcero from San José, Grecia, Alajuela and San Ramón.

CENTERS FOR DISEASE CONTROL MUSEUM

The COVID-19 pandemic transformed us all into reluctant students of infectious illnesses, but the true experts reside at the Centers for Disease Control and Prevention (CDC), headquartered in Atlanta. When news headlines warn of bird-borne illnesses, or TV shows like *The Last of Us* inspire new nightmares about fast-spreading zombie fungi, eyes turn to the CDC for reassurance about the security of global health.

The David J Sencer CDC Museum focuses on the agency's achievements in studying, treating and preventing disease, showcasing artefacts from retro quarantine signs to pedal-powered injection apparatus (all thoroughly decontaminated, we assume). Multimedia displays and timelines of medical milestones, like iron lungs and the elimination of polio, convey the swift march of scientific progress – along with the many challenges that lie ahead.

★ **THIS SMITHSONIAN AFFILIATE** is open Monday to Friday; entry is free.

BAY ISLANDS UNDERWATER MUSEUM

Tired of the same old humdrum museum routine? Are you over the informational headsets, long queues and crowds? Then pack a swimsuit and some flippers and head over to the Bay Islands Underwater Museum. This unique exhibition is located off the coast of Roatán, one of Honduras' picturesque Bay Islands. Shunning traditional exhibits for an experience filled with adventure, the museum leads snorkelling visitors into the glittering Caribbean waters, where they can discover a number of rather unique sunken treasures: Maya statues, Paya artefacts, Garifuna canoes, old anchors and even a Spanish galleon. Guides will fill you in on the background of these items before you hit the surf for your underwater scavenger hunt, and give you some background about colonisation in this part of the Americas and the subsequent fight for independence.

However, the experience isn't purely an historical one. The Bay Islands are known as one of the world's pre-eminent locations to observe coral reefs, and abundant wildlife thrives among the museum's installations. Brightly hued fish swim around the sunken artefacts, while golden starfish and striped shrimp move across the sandy ocean floor. Corals punctuate the seascape, and crabs duck in and out of their hiding spots.

* **AT THE TIME** of writing, travel was not advised to Honduras.

SALVATION MOUNTAIN

The life's work of Leonard Knight, Salvation Mountain is a living prayer in a desolate wilderness, as compellingly unique as it is utterly out of place. Born in Vermont in 1931, Knight was a drifter until a religious epiphany struck in 1967. By 1984, he had set to work, using his bare hands to build an adobe and straw mountain, set on a low mesa in the baking-hot Southern California desert near the Salton Sea. His simple mission was to share his religious fervour with the world, spelling it out in paint on his mountain – and it consumed him until his death in 2014. The result is a surreal merging of mountain and prayer book.

With its peak reaching just over 15m (49ft), the mountain face declares 'God is Love' over a massive red heart. Topped by a gleaming white cross and framed by painted waves that Knight called his 'Sea of Galilee', the mountain is coated with an estimated 37,8500 litres (83,258 gallons) of paint in a rainbow spectrum of trees, flowers, waterfalls and countless prayers.

I followed a yellow path, past a towering wall inscribed with the sinner's prayer and various biblical quotes, to the 'Hogan' – a circular room decorated eclectically with the cast-off detritus of the desert, and an homage to the local Indigenous people. Next I visited Knight's 'museum' of towering walls, held in place by a forest of surreally twisted, neon-painted trees, all winding towards heaven like giant fingers. I wandered through a maze of dead ends, which Knight said always brought the visitor back to God.

Finally, I climbed to the base of the mountain's cross for a panoramic view of the 45m/148ft-long monument and the surrounding graveyard of abandoned, prayer-covered vehicles. At the centre is the rusting truck that Knight called his home for 31 years.

Salvation Mountain is listed in the Congressional Record as a national treasure, and has appeared in several films. It's maintained by volunteers, some of whom live on-site, all of them eager to greet visitors and answer questions while soliciting donations of paint for the nonstop maintenance the monument requires. *–JAMES DORSEY*

* **SALVATION MOUNTAIN IS** just outside the town of Niland, which sits on Hwy 111.

GOD IS
LOVE
THE HOLY BIBLE
GOD
GODS HOLY BIBLE
GOD SO
ACTS 2:
38
SAY JESUS I'M
A SINNER PLEASE
COME UPON MY
BODY AND INTO
MY HEART
PLEASE KEEP OUT
PLEASE KEEP OUT

GEORGIA, USA

LUNCHBOX MUSEUM

Readers of a certain age might remember the days of toting lunch to school in a metal box, usually with a matching thermos tucked inside. If you want to see your old mealtime pal again, chances are you'll find it at the world's largest lunchbox collection in Columbus, Georgia. One of eight museums that comprise the Columbus Collective (all housed in a restored warehouse once used for tiles and marble), the lunchbox section displays some 5000 varied receptacles – from vintage pieces to more modern designs featuring pop-culture icons like *Star Trek*, *Peanuts*, *Strawberry Shortcake* and *Pac Man*. The other delightfully retro collections cover the Royal Crown soda company, Tom Huston peanuts, antique radios, local folk art and automobiles old and new.

● **THE COLLECTIONS ARE** open Monday to Saturday, 10am to 6pm.

BIG ISLAND, HAWAI'I

PLASTIC BEACH

A time-honoured Pacific melting pot, this stretch of coast on the Big Island's southeastern tip is officially called Kamilo Beach ('the swirling currents' in Hawaiian). A combination of powerful tides and trade winds once delivered all kinds of valuable flotsam to the ancient Hawaiians here, including logs from the Pacific Northwest to fashion into canoes. However, in recent years the ocean has been delivering a different bounty: astounding amounts of debris from the Great Pacific Garbage Patch – the world's largest accumulation of ocean plastic waste, covering an area of 1.6 million sq km (618,000 sq miles). Today, on what's known as Plastic Beach, you're likely to discover ephemera from every side of the ocean, not to mention a lesson on the wastefulness of humankind and the unrelenting power of nature.

● **THE BEACH IS** near Nā'ālehu, via a maze of sharp volcanic rock. Tread carefully or come by 4WD.

PETRIFIED LIGHTNING

At Great Sand Dunes National Park, craggy jewels of petrified lightning pepper the sand. Resembling charred tree branches or clumps of coral, these hunks of glass – known as fulgurites – look organic but somehow not of this Earth; no wonder, given they're quite literally heaven-sent. Fulgurites are born when lightning strikes sand and melts it at an unimaginable 28,000°C/50,400°F (many times hotter than the sun's surface), instantly creating knobbly works of art.

Great Sands' 604-sq-km (233-sq-mile) expanse of dune fields and mountains sits in Colorado's San Luis Valley, the largest alpine valley in the world; and many of the park's dunes – North America's tallest – have been forming for 400,000 years. These dunes endlessly shapeshift with the wind: pyramidal 'star dunes' evoke a mirage of ancient Egypt, while 'reversing dunes' – sculpted by the action of wind blowing in different directions – cast magical indigo shadows as the sun sets. The park's landscape is also a hot-spot for storms, especially on summer afternoons, when the dunes become a vast canvas for lightning to fry sand into fulgurites. Like high-voltage snowflakes, no two are alike: the electric current dissipates as it strikes the sand, branching off and zigzagging in a treelike pattern – rather like the infinite unfolding geometry of a fractal.

Look closely at the sand to spot them. Most fulgurites are less than 7cm (3in) in size, but they can be almost 1m (3ft) long, protruding from the sand like celestial spears that hurtled to Earth.

THE PARK IS in south-central Colorado, roughly four hours' drive from major airports in Denver (Colorado) and Albuquerque (New Mexico). Follow route advice on the National Parks Service website, instead of online mapping tools. Always leave fulgurites in the sand for others to enjoy.

CAVE OF THE CRYSTALS

If you were to journey deep below surface level at Chihuahua's Naica mine, descending some 300m (984ft) towards the centre of the Earth, you'd find yourself in a science-fiction-worthy cave of translucent, gargantuan crystals. Humans are dwarfed by glistening pillars – some up to 4m (13ft) thick – that crisscross the cavern like Escher staircases; other blocks of shorter obelisk-shaped shafts line the walls. Some say the cavern looks like a cathedral, others are reminded of Superman's icy lair – but everyone agrees that it is one of the most astounding spectacles on the planet.

Anyone who enters requires a helmet, a respirator and an ice-packed suit to protect against the 50°C (122°F) temperatures and high humidity – but even with the proper attire, humans can only survive in here for around 20 minutes. Unsurprisingly, the cave was closed to the public shortly after its discovery in 2000, when a mineworker snuck in and was roasted alive.

Some of the crystals are estimated to be around 500,000 years old and are likely the largest specimens ever discovered by humans. The mineral is selenite, a soft substance that's easily damaged – it can be scratched by a fingernail. The caves were naturally filled with water but were pumped dry by the mining company. When, or if, the mine floods the chambers again, the crystals will begin to grow anew, but they will also be lost to human sight and research, possibly forever.

ENTRY IS PROHIBITED to all but accredited (and suitably suited-up) scientists. Additionally, at the time of writing, travel was not advised to the state of Chihuahua.

THE SUPERSTITION MOUNTAINS

Far from the crowded trails that outdoor adventurers tend to flock to in the Greater Phoenix Area, lie the Superstition Mountains – a place steeped in mysterious history and dazzling desert beauty that is only about 64km (40 miles) away along Hwy 60.

The ancestral home of the Akimel O'odham and the White Mountain Apache people, the Superstitions are as gorgeous as they are wild. Towering 1829m (6000ft) above the Sonoran Desert, these craggy mountains were formed by volcanic activity millions of years ago; it's said their name came from the Akimel O'odham people, who spoke of disappearances, unexplained deaths, as well as a general fear of the mountains and the sounds that emerge from them. Today, people continue to claim they hear the mountains rumbling, emitting sounds that resemble deep rolling thunder. Geologists say these sounds stem from seismic activity that vibrates through the landscape.

Located within the Superstition Wilderness Area, comprising around 64,750 hectares (160,000 acres) of jutting mountains, towering saguaro cacti and rugged desert, the Superstitions are a delightful place of adventure. Paths such as the Fremont Saddle and Hieroglyphic Trail will take you to see ancient petroglyphs and waterfalls amid miles and miles of desert. Wherever the mountains take you, just make sure to bring enough refreshments for your trip, as trailheads may not have water fountains available.

* **MOBILE-PHONE SERVICE IN** the area is scarce, and in some places you'll need a car that can navigate unpaved roads.

THE SOURTOE COCKTAIL

The legend of the Sourtoe Cocktail begins in the 1920s, when rum runners Louie and Otto Linken were caught in a blizzard and Louie's toe became frostbitten. Fearing gangrene, the brothers amputated the afflicted digit using an axe and some rum (for anaesthesia and courage). To mark the event, they preserved the toe in a jar of booze.

Decades later, Captain Dick Stevenson found the jar and brought it to Dawson City's Sourdough Saloon. There he used the toe to garnish the drinks of those brave enough to join the 'Sourtoe Cocktail Club'. Today, visitors can become club members by gulping down a digit-embellished shot (but lips must touch the toe).

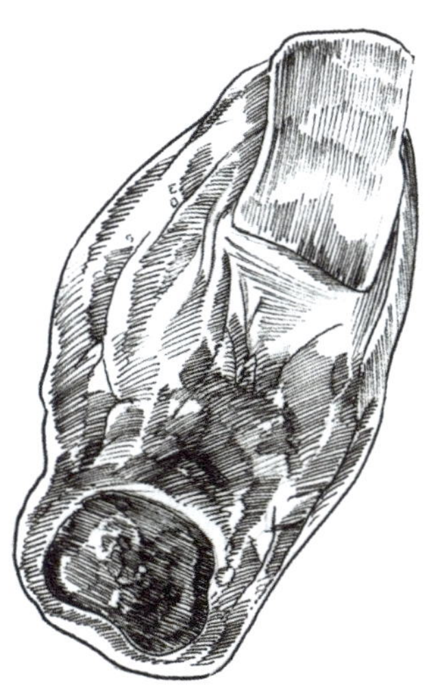

* **THE SOURDOUGH SALOON** is on the corner of Queen St and Second Ave in tiny Dawson City.

TANK TOWN USA

If you're in Morganton, Georgia, with an insatiable urge to destroy things with heavy machinery, head on over to Tank Town USA. Its motto is simple and accurately describes the fun to be had here: 'Drive Tanks, Crush Cars'. The main attraction is the tank-driving course, which you can work your way around – the end of the route is where the car-crushing action happens.

If you've always wanted to work on a building site, you can fulfil those dreams here as well – take a 18-tonne (20-ton) construction excavator for a spin and dig holes to your heart's content.

* **OPEN THURSDAY, SATURDAY** and Sunday (other times by reservation), from April to November.

MUSEO SUB- ACUÁTICO DE ARTE

Most art lovers pick up a museum audio-guide rather than a snorkelling mask – but the Museo Subacuático de Arte (MUSA) takes immersive art literally. Its galleries lie deep in the gin-clear waters of Isla Mujeres and Punta Nizuc off Cancún, where shoals of silvery fish flit past more than 500 permanent sculptures on the seafloor.

These life-sized figures raise their hands high, or slump despondently on the pearly sand. Creating them doesn't end when the sculptors – underwater art pioneer Jason deCaires Taylor among them – put away their chisels and casting moulds. After the artwork is lowered into the sea, colonies of marine-dwellers get to work: corals and sea anemones take up residence on the sculptures, softening their concrete features and making them one with the ocean. Lobsters make themselves at home inside an 8-tonne (9-ton) VW Beetle sculpture, and eels slither beneath praying figures.

This intermingling of art and nature is by design: MUSA was dreamed up as a way to draw visitors away from overvisited natural coral reefs. And the experience is almost euphoric: propel yourself with flippers to float above enigmatic figures like DeCaires Taylor's *Void* and *Gardener of Hope*, or Elier Amado Gil's meditative *Threshold*. In DeCaires Taylor's *The Silent Evolution*, 400 statues, many of them modelled on local people, stand up in protest to protect their seas – a message that lingers as you ponder your own effect on Mexico's fragile ecosystems.

SCULPTURES LOCATED 4M (13ft) deep are accessible to snorkellers (or can be viewed from glass-bottomed boats). Others, sunk 8m (26ft) deep, can only be reached by certified divers. MUSA offers tours of both. Make sure to review current travel advisories before planning a trip.

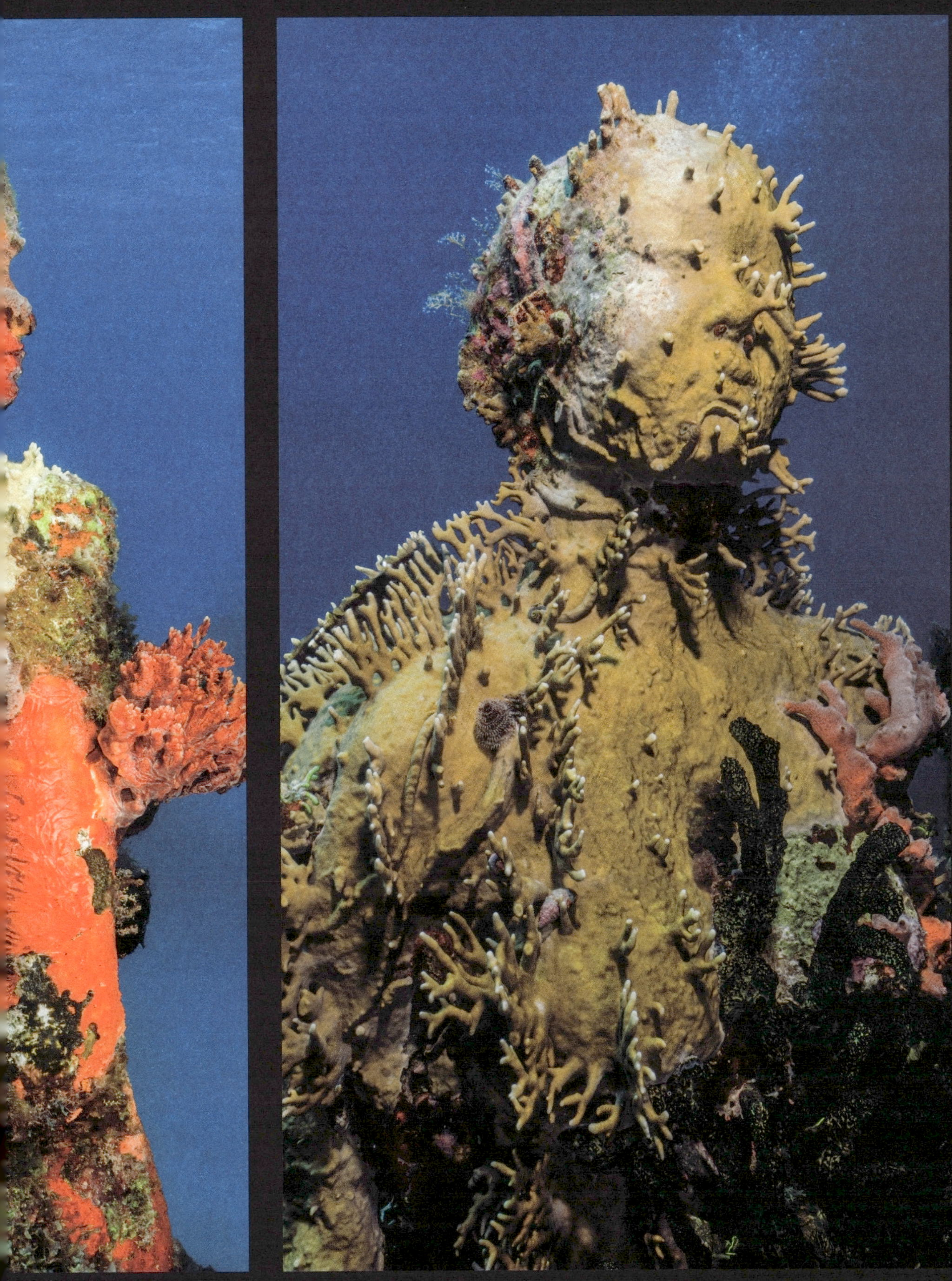

SOUTH AMERICA & ANTARCTICA

ANA KAI TANGATA

On the southwest coast of Rapa Nui, midnight-blue waves smash the shore and cast pearly foam onto the rocks. The island formed when three volcanoes fused together, and its explosive past is evident in the jagged lava shoreline, which is honeycombed with sea caves like 10m/33ft-high Ana Kai Tangata.

Its name is often translated as 'cave where men are eaten' and shortened to 'Cave of the Cannibals'. An alternative translation could be 'man-eating cave'.

Walk steadily down the stone steps into the cave and peer at paintings of sooty terns, still faintly visible on the ceiling. These migratory seabirds were believed to be sacred by devotees of Makemake, the chief god of Tangata Manu (Rapa Nui's bird-man cult); collecting the first tern egg of the season was a ritualistic competition for generations of islanders. The victor would be showered with gifts from other clans and win the honour of exclusive rights for his entire group to collect eggs all season.

• SEEING ENIGMATIC CAVES and Rapa Nui's famous *moai* (stone statues) doesn't come cheap or easy. Flights from Chile's capital, Santiago, reach Mataveri International Airport; visitors must fill out a registration form in advance.

GUINEA PIG LAST SUPPER

In the historic Catedral del Cuzco, completed in 1654 on Cuzco's Spanish-built main square, a painting depicts a classic biblical scene – with a uniquely Peruvian twist. In Leonardo da Vinci's iconic version, Jesus and his disciples sit around a feast of bread and wine; in *The Last Supper*, painted by Quechua painter Marcos Zapata in 1753, the plate at the centre of the table features a cooked guinea pig. Native to Peru, guinea pigs were consumed by the Inca and are still served in Cuzco restaurants today. Zapata's art frequently combines Christian themes with Indigenous culinary culture, most likely as a way of converting the Indigenous population.

● **THE CATHEDRAL IS** the main feature at Plaza de Armas. Make sure to review current travel advisories before planning a trip.

NAVE ESPACIAL DE VARGINHA

Varginha is South America's equivalent of Roswell, New Mexico. Ever since January 1996, when locals reported seeing UFOs and an alien creature ('5ft tall with a large head, thin body, V-shaped feet and red eyes'), the town has become a UFO pilgrimage site. Businesses cash in on the rumours of alien visitation, shops stock all sorts of *E.T.* souvenirs, and local media are ever keen to perpetuate the stories. In 2001, the town authorities devised a brilliant plan. They needed to construct a water tower, so they decided to disguise it in the shape of an enormous flying saucer. Christened the Nave Espacial de Varginha (Spaceship of Varginha), it looms 20m (66ft) above the town and lights up at night.

● **VARGINHA IS 400KM** (249 miles) northeast of Rio. The tower is on the junction of Praça Getúlio Vargas and Praça Mal Floriano. Make sure to review current travel advisories before planning a trip.

VILLA PUERTO EDÉN

Is this the rainiest place on the entire planet? Quite possibly. A tiny fishing village among the fjords of southern Chile, Villa Puerto Edén is drenched with precipitation, notching up nearly 6000mm (236in) a year. Because of all that water, roads would get washed away, so instead the locals – all 176 of them, according to the last census – get around town using pedestrian boardwalks or in their boats.

Not far from the southern tip of South America, the village is also one of the most isolated places on Earth, accessible only by sea. Public transport is not always straightforward: one local ferry company, Navimag, services Villa Puerto Edén as part of its four-day journey through the fjords.

When you arrive here, on the east coast of the enormous Isla Wellington, that long journey will seem worth it. (Provided, of course, you can see through the veils of rain.) What first hits you are the ramshackle but brightly painted houses and huts overlooking the seafront. Looming behind them are mountains of the Parque Nacional Bernardo O'Higgins, which remain snowcapped even in summer.

Villa Puerto Edén is home to the world's last surviving members of the Kawésqar people. There are only a handful still here; the last repositories of their language and culture.

* **NAVIMAG OFFERS A** four-day ferry service to Villa Puerto Edén from Puerto Montt (on Fridays) and from Puerto Natales (on Tuesdays).

CAÑO CRISTALES

One of South America's most dynamic natural-art shows unfolds deep within one of Colombia's best-protected and most pristine national parks. Located 280km (174 miles) from Bogotá near the isolated town of La Macarena, Parque Nacional Natural Sierra de La Macarena is home to Caño Cristales, a waterfall-splashed river that turns into a 'liquid rainbow' between the wet and dry seasons. For much of the year, this remote crystal-clear river looks no different than other ordinary waterways. But between July and November, the water levels are just right for the aquatic plant *Macarenia clavigera* to bloom beneath the surface, turning the landscape into a technicolor cabernet.

Witnessing the kaleidoscopic Caño Cristales is a rare opportunity. Only Indigenous locals knew about the so-called 'river of five colours' until the late 1960s; and until 2009, the entire region was inaccessible, due to FARC (Revolutionary Armed Forces of Colombia) activity. Now, a restricted number of people (around 200) are allowed to enter the park each day, but only all under the careful watch of hired guides from official tour companies.

● **AT THE TIME** of writing, travel was not advised to Colombia.

VIADUCT PETROBRAS

Is this the ultimate white elephant? Back in the 1960s the plan was to build a high-speed motorway between Rio de Janeiro and Santos. One section, the 370m/1214ft-long Viaduct Petrobras, was completed – but when government officials changed the route, the roads either end of it never were. Now, disconnected, abandoned and alone, this huge elevated concrete roadway looms 40m (131ft) above the jungle floor, while plant life gradually swallows it up. It may have been designed for motor vehicles, but nowadays the traffic is mostly climbers and bungee jumpers looking for somewhere unusual to practise their sports. Ladders link the jungle to the roadway.

● **THE VIADUCT IS** just southwest of Caraguatatuba. Small roads take you close, but the last stretch is by foot or 4WD. Make sure to review current travel advisories before planning a trip.

SWING AT THE END OF THE WORLD

High up in the Ecuadorian jungle, a treehouse perches precariously at the edge of a canyon. The Casa del Árbol is actually a seismic observation station built to keep an eye on Tungurahua, the active volcano next to it. Local Carlos Sánchez vowed to keep watch over the valley, after his home and livestock were spared during a 1999 eruption that sent ash and rocks thundering down the slopes. His swings offer the best bird's-eye view of the valley. Suspended by ropes hanging from a tree, the swings launch daredevils high into the air for head-spinning views of the canyon floor... and perhaps a glimpse of an erupting volcano as they swing over its lip.

● **THE SWING IS** 10.5km (6.5 miles) up a steep, winding mountain road from the town of Baños. Make sure to review current travel advisories before planning a trip.

SNAKE ISLAND

If you're afraid of snakes, look away now. Ilha da Queimada Grande, off the coast of Brazil, is home to the world's entire population of golden lancehead pit vipers – several thousand of them. Since the island comprises just 43 hectares (106 acres), that averages out at about one snake every square metre, each armed with a particularly fast-acting venom designed to swiftly take down the birds it preys on. But despite the many reptilian residents here, golden lanceheads are critically endangered; São Paulo's Instituto Butantan (p270) hopes that their breeding programme will usher in a cold-blooded baby boom. No wonder the Brazilian government bans access to everyone except its navy and accredited researchers. Illegal wildlife smugglers sometimes sneak in, in search of snakes to sell on the black market. (Does this remind you of *Jurassic Park* yet?)

Thousands of years ago, Snake Island, as it has been nicknamed in English, was attached to the mainland, until rising sea levels eventually cut it off by a distance of 32km (20 miles), allowing the golden lanceheads to multiply with abandon and evolve their particularly lethal venom. Since then they have survived by slithering up the trees in search of birds.

The island's Brazilian name translates roughly as 'Big Burning Island', since attempts were once made to clear land for a banana plantation. In the early 1900s a lighthouse was built, but following the deaths of three keepers from snake bites, the light was automated in 1920.

● **THE ISLAND LIES** some 150km (93 miles) offshore of São Paulo, but it's off-limits to all but certified researchers.

GLOBAL VAMPIRE HUNTING

Vampires occupy the threshold between life and death, love and terror. Whether you prefer them brooding in black lace, coffin-bound in a Gothic castle or greedily devouring human souls, we know all the right places to look.

LOUISIANA, USA

1. NEW ORLEANS

If vampires have a modern-day HQ, it's New Orleans, where a subculture of 'sanguinarian' (blood-drinking) vampires look for volunteer victims. Locals say it began when an early-20th-century resident, suspiciously wealthy and handsome Jacques St Germain, was accused of biting a woman on the neck. Hang around the French Quarter's Vampire Cafe for long enough and you're bound to meet one...

WHITBY, ENGLAND

2. WHITBY ABBEY

When Bram Stoker put quill to paper to write *Dracula* (1897), eerie Whitby Abbey struck him as a perfect setting – and tales of a local shipwreck inspired a climactic scene in the novel. The vampires live on at dark-hearted Whitby Goth Weekend.

3

4

8

10

GLOBAL VAMPIRE HUNTING

ORAVSKÝ PODZÁMOK, SLOVAKIA

3. ORAVA CASTLE

Long before Lily-Rose Depp writhed in blood-drenched ecstasy in the 2024 movie, the 1922 silent film *Nosferatu* made audiences tremble. The count's lair is Romanesque Orava Castle, dramatically perched on a 520m/1706ft-high limestone spire.

WASHINGTON, USA

4. FORKS

In her *Twilight* books, author Stephenie Meyer made this sleepy logging town the home of glittering vampires and werewolves. But this area has held stories of people transforming into wolves long before that series. Among the people of the Quileute Tribe, their origin story tells of two wolves turning into humans.

AREFU, ROMANIA

5. POIENARI CITADEL

Castles throughout Romania clamour to claim a link with Vlad 'the Impaler' Țepeș, but Poienari is the real deal. Wallachia's warlord chose this crag as a lookout, and its walls offer the most authentic glimpse of the real Dracula's military prowess.

CALIFORNIA, USA

6. BELA LUGOSI'S GRAVE

With mesmeric eyes and a velvety Hungarian accent, Bela Lugosi was immortalised in *Dracula* (1931). At his final resting place in the Greater Los Angeles Holy Cross Cemetery, Lugosi lies buried in a vampire's cloak.

WEST KALIMANTAN, INDONESIA

7. PONTIANAK

Pale skin, blood-smeared clothing and the odour of death all tell of the Pontianak, a long-haired female vampire. The Indonesian city was named for her after 18th-century noble Syarif Abdurrahman Alkadrie battled horrifying wraiths here.

PRAGUE, CZECHIA

8. OLŠANY CEMETERY

If you're extra clumsy as you walk between tombs in Czechia's largest cemetery, blame Krvavé koleno (Bloody Knee): he was bitten during a bar fight and still lashes out at passerby, licking blood from their scuffed knees.

RHODE ISLAND, USA

9. MERCY BROWN GRAVESTONE

During a 19th-century tuberculosis outbreak, rumours swirled that the undead were returning. Panicked exhumations followed, and young Mercy Brown's body was deemed suspiciously vampiric. Mercy was burned to ashes, which were fed to her ailing brother (no, this didn't save him).

ČACHTICE, SLOVAKIA

10. ČACHTICE CASTLE

Elizabeth Báthory was accused of murdering maids and bathing in their blood, or was it a smear campaign against a noble who owned land and educated young women? Explore the ruins of her mid-13th-century castle and contemplate the patriarchy's nightmare...

MUSEO DEL CEREBRO

An unprepossessing building down a backstreet behind Lima's Institute of Neurological Science hides a remarkable collection. More than 3000 neatly labelled, formaldehyde-filled jars line the walls, the brains inside them displaying damage caused by diseases; ranging from neurological disorders and substance abuse to tumours, strokes, Alzheimer's and even Creutzfeldt–Jakob disease (the human variant of mad cow disease, officially known by the snappy name of bovine spongiform encephalopathy). Neuropathologist Diana Rivas oversees the collection and performs autopsies in the same building, acquiring more specimens. While most visitors tend to be neurology students and academics, Rivas also educates the general public about preventable diseases by letting them see the effects up close.

* **THE MUSEUM IS** in a fairly rough part of town. It's best to take a taxi. Make sure to review current travel advisories before planning a trip.

ANTIOQUIA, COLOMBIA

PIEDRA DEL PEÑOL

Partially covered in sparse greenery, a giant stone rises steeply from the verdant, hilly grounds around the small town of Guatapé, reaching a height of nearly 200m (656ft). Worshipped by the Indigenous Tahamies people centuries ago, the monolith was first officially scaled in 1954 by a group of friends; the five-day climb was made using a series of boards wedged into the single cleft in the otherwise smooth rock. Today, visitors can ascend the rock and the lookout tower at the summit using the 649-step masonry staircase wedged into the crack. The show-stopping vista from the summit – a series of lakes and islands – was created when the area was dammed in the 1970s.

* **AT THE TIME** of writing, travel was not advised to Colombia.

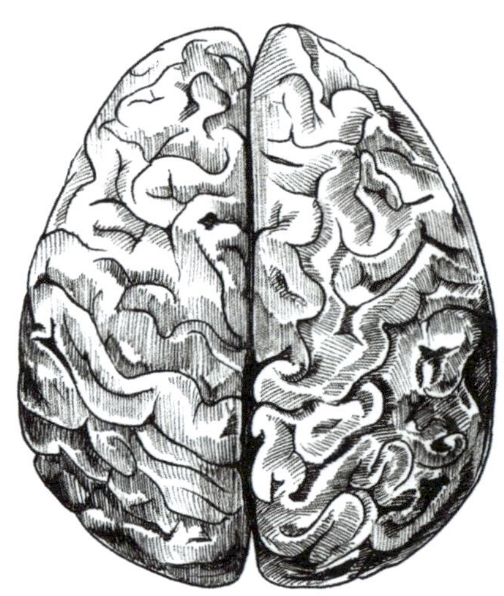

USHUAIA TIME CAPSULE

You'd think the end of the world would be lonely. But it's always busy in Ushuaia, in the Tierra del Fuego archipelago. This southernmost city on Earth is a gateway to Antarctica. Cruise-ship passengers descend to wander the town; adventurous types come and go from boating and hiking excursions.

I'd been on a boat all morning, exploring the archipelago's cormorant colonies and snapping photos. Back on dry land, it was starting to snow. I was hurrying along when a sculpture caught my eye.

● **THE CAPSULE IS** on Plaza 25 de Mayo, by the boat harbour between the taxi stand and artisan market.

Retro and geometric, the monument rose up from a plaza like a miniature pyramid. But it was the inscription that stopped me in my tracks: 'Do not open until October 2nd 2492'.

2492? It seemed like a mistake. I stepped closer to read the plaque. It was a time capsule, sealed in 1992 and intended to be opened in 2492, 1000 years after Christopher Columbus arrived in the Americas. Inside were six laser video discs of Argentinian TV shows, and hundreds of written messages addressed to future citizens. The technology would certainly be obsolete by the time the capsule was opened. The thoughts expressed in the messages seemed more intriguing – what did people expect for the future? For Tierra del Fuego's Indigenous groups, the past centuries had been tumultuous. The arrival of European settlers signalled the end of the Yaghan or Yámana, the nomadic people who inhabited the archipelago. The last surviving full-blooded Yámana, Christina Calderón – who lived across the Chilean border in Puerto Williams – passed away in 2022, aged 93.

Calderón was the last speaker of the Yámana language. When she died, she took untold stories with her; a certain chapter of the present officially became the past. What would Ushuaia's contemporary residents have to say to those who will live here hundreds of years down the line? I'll never know – only time, a lot of time, will tell.

–BRIDGET GLEESON

MORAY

In a remote part of the hilly Sacred Valley sits a perfect amphitheatre of grass-covered terraced rings. Left behind by the Inca, its exact purpose had long baffled archaeologists. Compared to the sophisticated masonry and elaborate stone cities the Inca left elsewhere, these concentric terraces seem simple – but are in fact ingenious. Their design, their depth, variation in size and positioning in relation to the sun and wind all seem to suggest that they may have been an agricultural research station. The subtly varying climatic conditions on every terrace have resulted in the creation of different microclimates that correspond to varied growing conditions across the Inca Empire. At its height, this empire encompassed a huge swathe of South America, from the coast and jungle of Ecuador and the Peruvian highlands to the lakes, desert and mountains of Chile, with thousands upon thousands of subjects who required sustenance.

With a 15°C (59°F) variation between the top and bottom terraces, and soil samples proven to have been brought from different parts of Peru, it is likely that the Inca – remarkable agriculturalists that they were – used the terraces to test the growing prowess of different crops under varying climatic conditions, using modification and hybridisation to adapt potato, maize, quinoa, sweet potato and amaranth to make them suitable for human consumption.

COME TO MORAY either by taxi from Maras village, 5km (3 miles) away, or by guided day-tour from Cuzco. Make sure to review current travel advisories before planning a trip.

GRUTA DO LAGO AZUL

As we descend the crude stone staircase into the subterranean depths studded with stalactites and stalagmites, our guide explains that, most likely, no human had ever set foot inside this grotto until a member of the Terena Tribe stumbled upon it by accident in 1924. As we descend further, my jaw drops as I stare down into a startlingly blue pool. The water is crystal-clear but the pool – one of the largest flooded cavities on Earth – is so deep it seems bottomless. In 1992, a Franco-Brazilian diving team explored its 70m (230ft) depths and discovered that the bottom was rich in prehistoric animal remains, from sabre-toothed tigers to giant sloths. *–ANNA KAMINSKI*

THE CAVE IS 19km (12 miles) from Bonito and access is by two-hour tour between 7am and 2pm; most lodgings in Bonito organise tours. Closed-toed walking shoes are mandatory. Make sure to review current travel advisories before planning a trip.

WALL OF TEARS

The very stones on Isla Isabela have restless energy. Formed when lava from six shield volcanoes bled into one, the island – the largest in the Galápagos archipelago – is one of the most volcanically active points on Earth. But its human history, too, is ill at ease.

Hundreds of prisoners from mainland Ecuador were shipped to Isabela's notorious penal colony. Between 1945 and 1959, the inmates were ordered to construct a 100m (328ft) wall enclosing the compound. Hauling the volcanic basalt and chipping it into pieces with primitive tools was a Sisyphean task, designed to ruin their bodies and crush their spirits.

The wall – known as El Muro de las Lágrimas (the Wall of Tears) – is now the only thing that remains of the penal colony. Locals say the stones moan and scream; they're the last witnesses to the suffering of those who died in the brutal camp.

FLY TO ISLA Isabela from Baltra and San Cristóbal, or catch a ferry from San Cristóbal. Many travellers rent a bike and cycle the potholed, uneven route to the wall from Villamil (6km/4 miles). Make sure to review current travel advisories before planning a trip.

TEQUENDAMA FALLS MUSEUM

Overlooking the eponymous 157m/515ft-high falls, this haunted-hotel-turned-museum has worn many hats over the years. It began its existence in 1923 as a luxurious fin-de-siècle French-style mansion, designed by architect Carlos Arturo Tapias. For years it attracted the upper strata of Bogotá society with its superb location and lush surroundings. During the 1950s, it was set to be transformed into an 18-storey resort hotel, but expansion plans were shelved. As the Bogotá River feeding the falls gradually became more and more polluted with raw sewage from the capital, the stream of tourists slowed down to a trickle and, in the early 1990s, the hotel was abandoned and left to fall into genteel decay and disrepair. It acquired a reputation as a

haunted house after its picturesque yet precarious setting drew a number of unhappy souls here to shuffle off this mortal coil by throwing themselves off the cliff.

In more recent years, the mansion has been restored, thanks to a collaborative venture led by the Institute of Natural Sciences of the National University of Colombia and the Ecological Farm Foundation of Porvenir. In 2013, it was transformed into a museum of biodiversity and culture, coinciding with clean-up efforts aimed at rejuvenating the Bogotá River and protecting the fragile ecosystems surrounding the building.

● **AT THE TIME** of writing, travel was not advised to Colombia.

PARQUE NACIONAL DOS LENÇÓIS MARANHENSES

At first glance, it seems a mirage. A translucent, postcard-perfect lagoon surrounded by towering sand dunes as far as the eye can see. But then the splashdown reveals this otherworldly landscape is far from fantasy. As I dip below the surface, the cool and calming sensation is a travel moment – those minutes of elusive wonderment we all seek as we traverse the globe – and it feels like everything but an optical illusion.

Brazil's Parque Nacional dos Lençóis Maranhenses, a 1550-sq-km (598-sq-mile) expanse of cinematic sand-scapes, is a natural treasure. Located in the far northeastern state of Maranhão, it is the kind of place travel dreams are made of, a transcendental protected park of blanketing white dunes only broken up by the inviting cerulean lagoons that pepper the sandy hills between March and September (there is almost no vegetation whatsoever). From the air, the sweeping landscape gives the appearance of rolling bedsheets (*lençóis* in Portuguese), pitching across the world's most picturesque bed. From the ground, a desert-scape unravels into the horizon in every direction.

Access the park from the nearby town of Barreirinhas, a five-hour drive from the city of São Luís, from where open-sided 4WD bus tours hit some of the park's biggest lagoons, Lagos Azul (Blue) and Bonita (Beautiful). Needless to say, this is not the best way to experience the park. I opted instead for a private tour from the Rancho do Buna guesthouse in the charming sand village of Atins, a 1½-hour boat ride along the Rio Preguiças from Barreirinhas.

Everywhere you look, the landscape is alarmingly similar, yet my guide knew the park backwards and forward. We visited a series of secluded lagoons far away from the tour buses and tourists on day trips, and afforded me the opportunity to immerse myself in this aquatic Eden once mistaken for a mirage. When I resurface, I'm lost, surrounded by nothing and no one. Paradise found. *–KEVIN RAUB*

CISNE BRANCO RUNS buses from Saõ Luís to Barreirinhas, the gateway to the park. Make sure to review current travel advisories before planning a trip.

SUCRE, BOLIVIA

PARQUE CRETÁCICO

Sixty-eight million years ago, a vast ocean inlet reached as far inland as Sucre in Bolivia, with dinosaurs such as the Tyrannosaurus rex, as well as hadrosaur and ceratops species, leaving their imprints in the soft clay shore. Today, 5055 footprints turned to stone can be seen on a near-vertical cliff of Cal Orck'o, the most impressive of which belong to a baby T-rex. Apart from the viewing trail that runs alongside the cliff – close enough to see the footprints but far enough away to protect visitors from unstable sections of the Cal Orck'o – the world's largest dinosaur-track site includes the skeletons of a T-rex and a carnotaurus, as well as sculptures of other dinosaurs in dramatic battle mode.

* **PARQUE CRETÁCICO IS** 5km (3 miles) outside Sucre, accessible by bus or taxi. Make sure to review current travel advisories before planning a trip.

CÓRDOBA, ARGENTINA

THE FOREST GUITAR

The young couple who dreamt up this project – a massive 'sculpture' of a guitar, 1km (0.6 miles) long and crafted from thousands of cypress and eucalyptus trees – never saw the result. That's because Graciela Yraizoz, the woman who conceived the idea, died of a brain aneurysm in 1977, at the age of 25. In homage to his late wife, farmer Pedro Martín Ureta undertook the task himself. With the help of their children, he strategically planted 7000 trees. Why the guitar? It was Graciela's favourite instrument. And why hasn't its creator ever seen the finished product? Ureta is afraid to fly – but he's happy with the aerial photos he's seen of his masterpiece.

* **THE FOREST GUITAR** is in the province of Córdoba. It is sometimes visible on flights between Buenos Aires and Mendoza.

CAMPANÓPOLIS

The year 1976 was a difficult one in Argentina. It marked the start of a brutal military dictatorship that would grip the nation for the better part of a decade. It was also the year that the Argentinian businessperson Antonio Campana was diagnosed with terminal throat cancer. It's no wonder, given the grim circumstances, that the self-made millionaire decided to abandon reality and build a fantasy world on an 80-hectare (198-acre) plot of land outside Buenos Aires. Campana made his fortune in the supermarket business; he had no training in architecture. But that didn't stop him from dreaming up the plans for a whimsical, fairy-tale village – nor did a legal battle over the land he'd purchased prevent him from bringing his visions to life. Sourcing materials from salvage auctions – doors, gates and fences as well as typewriters, an old elevator and metal scraps from discontinued railroad lines – he went to work on the construction of Campanópolis.

The doctors gave Campana five years to live, but he survived another 24. He devoted all of it to his enterprise: a medieval-style village with cobblestone streets, fountains, towers, a windmill and an artificial lake. Right up until his death in 2008, Campana continued developing his dream, planting more than 100,000 trees and bringing in myriad quirky antiques. Today, his sons maintain his unfinished masterpiece.

* **CAMPANÓPOLIS IS IN** González Catán. It's best to drive or take a taxi. Guided tours are available (book in advance).

BIZARRE BRAZIL

BRAZIL

SÃO PAULO, RIO DE JANEIRO, NOVA FRIBURGO, BELO HORIZONTE, PARQUE NACIONAL DAS EMAS & PETROLÂNDIA

RIO, SÃO PAULO, Belo Horizonte and Campo Grande (a common starting point for all-inclusive safaris to Parque Nacional das Emas), are well connected by plane. Tours of old Petrolândia start in the modern city. Make sure to review current travel advisories before planning a trip.

With kaleidoscopic art scenes, diverse culinary traditions and thousands of animals found nowhere else on Earth, Brazil has endless curiosities for visitors. Less globally well-known are the country's intrigues of history, from past plagues to dam-flooded towns, as well as the many enclaves of outsider art. With huge distances to cover, you could easily spend a year exploring South America's largest country and still leave craving more – so the only question is where to begin…

BIZARRE BRAZIL

INSTITUTO BUTANTAN, *SÃO PAULO*

When an outbreak of bubonic plague gripped the port of Santos in 1899, São Paulo's scientific community switched into crisis mode and established this biomedical centre to pump out antibody serums. Today the Instituto Butantan is a leafy science park, where the secretions of venomous snakes are milked for antivenom; pay your respects to these heroic serpents at the *reptário*.

MUSEU DE IMAGENS DO INCONSCIENTE, *RIO DE JANEIRO*

Creative expression is good for our mental health. It's uncontroversial today, but this was a radical idea when psychiatrist Nise da Silveira first proposed art therapy instead of 'treatments' like solitary confinement. Based on Jungian principles, she hoped that patients could channel their innermost thoughts into art. Many of their outpourings are now displayed in the Museu de Imagens do Inconsciente (Museum of Images from the Unconscious).

JARDIM DO NÊGO, *NOVA FRIBURGO*

Big frogs, exhibitionist mermaids and goggle-eyed toddlers all begin life as handfuls of wet clay at these sculpture gardens west of Nova Friburgo. Tripping along the forested pathways is like a portal into the joyful mind of the artist, Geraldo Simplicio. His moss-coated creations wink, grimace and grin with glee – smiles are guaranteed, selfies are inevitable.

PEANUT STREET, *BELO HORIZONTE*

Leave your car in neutral on Rua do Amendoim (Peanut St), in Belo Horizonte's southeasterly Mangabeiras neighbourhood, and it won't roll down – it will appear to stubbornly climb uphill. Naysayers claim that the curvature of the hill produces an optical illusion, obstructing the horizon and feeding our brains perspective-distorting visual cues. We say try it anyway and enjoy a fantastical, fleeting moment, where gravity seems optional.

BIOLUMINESCENT TERMITE MOUNDS, *PARQUE NACIONAL DAS EMAS*

At night, the tropical savannah of west-central Brazil resembles a neon cityscape. The termite mounds look like sparkling skyscrapers, in which every tiny window is lit up bright. These bioluminescent towers can be as tall as 7m (23ft), and their inhabitants are clever imposters; not termites but click beetle larvae, who beckon to potential prey with alluring glints of green. Don't look directly into the light...

SUBMERGED CHURCH, *PETROLÂNDIA*

The concrete skeleton of a church is the only visible remainder of Velha Petrolândia. The population were forcibly relocated before the city was drowned by the São Francisco River upon the completion of the 4700m/15,420ft-long Luiz Gonzaga Dam. The Igreja Submersa do Sagrado Coração de Jesus (Submerged Church of the Sacred Heart of Jesus) pokes out from the water, a symbol of the lost city and a reminder of the cost of 'progress'.

PREVIOUS PAGE: Termite mounds in Parque Nacional das Emas glimmer after dark

THIS PAGE: A church drowned by dam-released waters in Petrolândia

NAZCA LINES

The little plane judders along the short runway of tiny Nazca Airport and takes off. Soon we're high above the ring of greenery that surrounds Nazca's dusty cluster of streets, flying over bare hills and vast desert. However, the desert is not featureless. Looking down, we can see ruler-straight lines etched into the stony ground, some converging and crossing over before disappearing into the distance. Seen from above, these roads to nowhere are longer than any airplane runway.

Then the animals come into view: a monkey with an intricately curved tail, a hummingbird with a long beak, a spider as big as the Empire State Building, a bird, a tree, a lizard. Their limbs are perfectly proportioned, the lines perfectly straight. We are glued to the windows in awe as the plane twists this way and that, circling above each giant figure. Who drew these enormous animals? Who etched those straight lines into the surface of the desert? How? Why?

First brought to public attention in the 1930s, when commercial pilots began flying over Peru, the Nazca Lines – a series of miles-long straight lines, geometric shapes and stylised animal figures scattered over some 500 sq km (193 sq miles) of the parched Nazca Plain – have posed a puzzle to archaeologists and conspiracy theorists alike. It's believed that the geoglyphs were constructed by the ancient Nazca people who flourished here from around 200 BCE to 600 CE, and made by removing earth and rust-coloured rocks from the surface of the desert, exposing 30cm/12in-wide lines of light-coloured sand beneath. The designs have remained largely intact for up to 2000 years, due to lack of rain, wind and erosion.

How the ancient designers managed to create such straight lines and perfectly proportioned animals remains a mystery – as does their purpose. Theories abound: that the straight lines are ancient runways for alien spaceships, or that the animals are part of a giant astronomical calendar. Most recent theories suggest that the animal and bird images either represented astrological phases or the totems of different Nazca clans. As for the lines and trapezoids, it's possible that they were used in rituals to beg the gods for water in one of the driest parts of Peru.

–ANNA KAMINSKI

• **BEST VIEWED FROM** the air, the Nazca Lines can also be seen from the mirador (viewing tower) 20km (12 miles) outside Nazca. Make sure to review current travel advisories before planning a trip.

VILLA EPECUÉN

It's been compared to Atlantis or Pompeii – but let's go back to the beginning. Geographically speaking, Epecuén never seemed a likely pick for a luxurious getaway: the village was located in the outskirts of the province of Buenos Aires, hundreds of miles away from the capital, on the road to nowhere in particular. But the resort was set on the shores of one of the saltiest lakes in the world. From the village's foundation in the 1920s through its 1970s heyday, the healing waters of Lago Epecuén drew a steady stream of vacationers; in summer, they'd arrive by train, checking into their hotels or enjoying a leisurely lunch before going for a dip in the lake.

That was before a rare and catastrophic natural event occurred, permanently altering the fate of the once-peaceful retreat. In 1985, weather conditions over the lake caused a *seiche*, or standing wave, that broke the dam. The saline waters slowly swallowed the town, submerging the streets, relegating hundreds of businesses and homes to the floor of a deep, salty lake.

Villa Epecuén was underwater; salvaging what little they could, everyone left. Fast-forward to 2009. The waters finally receded, exposing a damp ghost-town of broken buildings and dead trees. The otherworldly concrete shells of the underwater village – ice-cream parlours, hotels, nightclubs – continue to fascinate archaeologists and photographers alike. But of the original residents, only one returned – Pablo Novak, who moved back to his home in 2009, living here as Villa Epecuén's sole resident until his death, aged 94, in 2024. *–BRIDGET GLEESON*

THE RUINS OF Villa Epecuén are near the town of Carhué, which is an eight-hour bus ride from Buenos Aires.

RAPA NUI (EASTER ISLAND), CHILE

RAPA NUI (EASTER ISLAND), CHILE

THE NAVEL OF THE WORLD

Remote Rapa Nui will take your heart and your soul in a few days. One of the most isolated places on Earth, this tiny speck of land is blessed with an extraordinary array of archaeological sites. Apart from the iconic *moai* (giant statues) that are scattered amid an eerie landscape, you'll also be mesmerised by the so-called Navel of the World, a perfectly round-shaped stone that lies on the island's north coast. Local legend claims that Polynesian supreme ruler (and father of the Rapa Nui people) Hotu Matu'a himself brought this stone here, symbolising the navel of the world. It's magnetic – when a compass is placed on the rock it loses its direction.

● **GET HERE BY** bike, car or scooter from the island's main town, Hanga Roa. Access to the site is free.

ANTIOQUIA, COLOMBIA

LA CUEVA DEL ESPLENDOR

In the green mountains high above the little town of Jardín, a river runs through the aptly named Cueva del Esplendor (Cave of Splendour). The roof of the cavern has been worn down by the gushing stream over the centuries, and a luminescent waterfall cascades through the hole it carved out from the rock. In recent years, this comely cave has become a popular destination for hikers and equestrians, with sweaty travellers making a beeline for the deep, refreshing pool at the base of the waterfall as the reward for their exertion. Getting here is half the fun, with beautiful views of the surrounding mountains en route, followed by a steep scramble down a riverbed trail to the cave itself.

● **AT THE TIME** of writing, travel was not advised to Colombia.

CAPILLA DE MÁRMOL

We're hardwired to find the colour blue irresistible. As the rarest colour in nature, blue immediately catches our eye; during the daytime, blue wavelengths boost our mood and invigorate our bodies.

No wonder it's so hard to look away from Chile's sky-coloured Capilla de Mármol (Marble Caves). Powder-blue and silver patterns dance across the stone, and natural archways are mirrored in the bright teal waters. Buffed and polished over 6000 years by waves in Lago General Carrera, cave walls look like a swirling sky painted by Van Gogh.

The gigantic glacial lake straddles 1850 sq km (714 sq miles) across Chile and Argentina, but the Capilla de Mármol are the region's masterpiece. The marble formed when tectonic shifts drove limestone deep underground. Baked by the Earth's subterranean pressure cooker, the rock crystallised into marble, and impurities transformed into hallucinogenic patterns that ripple across the surface. Meanwhile, brisk winds were churning up waves in the lake (to the Tehuelche people, its name is Chelenko; literally 'stormy waters'). The lapping swells slowly carved the marble – first creating smooth, undulating shapes, and eventually tunnels and cathedral-like chambers.

Like all great beauties, the Capilla de Mármol are capricious. Springtime (September to November) is a palette of cyan and baby blue because of lower water levels; by summer (December to February), after the glacial melt, the lake swells and deepens to ocean-blue.

THE LAKESIDE TOWN of Puerto Río Tranquilo is the main jumping-off point for boat tours of the caves. Guided kayak excursions are even better: you can dip in and out of the larger caverns and experience this bolt-from-the-blue up close.

FRENCHMAN'S PASS

The Caribbean's past is full of ghosts: the arrival of European colonisers led to the decimation of native populations, while pirates raided coast after coast – and ships moved millions of enslaved people through the region in gruesome conditions, delivering them to horrific fates. The history of Aruba mirrors that of its neighbours: originally settled by the Caquetio Indigenous people (part of the Arawak Tribe), Aruba was claimed by Spain in 1499 and, in 1513, the native population was enslaved and taken to Hispaniola. Indigenous people from the Venezuelan mainland began to migrate to the island after the Spanish abandoned it (there was no gold), and the Dutch West India Company took control in 1636.

Frenchman's Pass is the name given to a narrow stretch of land above Spanish Lagoon, a place with a scenic ambience at odds with its deadly history. According to island lore, French pirates attempted to invade Aruba in 1620, but met fierce resistance here from Indigenous residents. The pirates tried to drive their opponents away by laying fires to smoke them out of a nearby cave; instead, the smoke from the fire asphyxiated them. Locals say that the cries of the Indigenous people who died here can still be heard at night, and reports of paranormal activity range from glowing balls of light to malfunctioning cars. Take the canopy-covered road through Frenchman's Pass to discover this eerily beautiful place and ponder its chilling history.

● **TAKE RTE 1** south out of Oranjestad. Turn left at Rte 4, then right on the road just past Rooi Bosal.

DOCK OF SOULS

The Ancient Greek legend of Charon – the ferryman who transported dead souls across the River Styx to the underworld – is well known. Less famous is the story of Chile's ferryman, *Tempilcahue*; according to ancient Mapuche lore, he also transported dead souls to the afterlife.

Chilean artist Marcelo Orellana Rivera paid homage to this story by building a huge wooden sculpture, *Muelle de las Almas (Dock of Souls)*, on a promontory of the island of Chiloé in southern Chile. It's a curved pier that stretches off the edge of a cliff, looking out across the Pacific Ocean. Sit here at sunset to absorb the superbly cinematic landscape – an appropriately glorious place from which to depart to another realm.

DRIVE SOUTH FROM the village of Cucao and park as close as possible. Make the final 45-minute hike on foot.

CATEDRAL DE SAL

Colombia's salt cathedral, one of only three in the world, reeked of tourist trap to me. But as I descended 180m (590ft) below ground into this otherworldly house of worship carved from 250,000 tonnes (275,600 tons) of salt, I quickly stood corrected. This stunning, dramatically lit sanctuary was a moving marvel. Ambling along the 14 small and maudlin chapels – each representing a Station of the Cross from Jesus' final journey – delivered an amazing passage through exquisite religious symbolism and mining triumph. If there is a God, he surely had a hand in the creation of the central nave (the world's largest underground church), where a mammoth cross, lit from head to toe, casts an unforgettable, ethereal glow. *–KEVIN RAUB*

AT THE TIME of writing, travel was not advised to Colombia.

VALE DA LUA

It has taken millions of years and trillions of litres of water to sculpt the beautiful rock formations at Vale da Lua (Moon Valley), on Brazil's São Miguel River. Stretching along a 1km (0.6 mile) course of water, just beyond the southern edge of the Parque Nacional da Chapada dos Veadeiros, is a bizarre-looking series of natural rock formations, caves, waterfalls, pools and crevices. It's a bit like a waterpark, but without the screaming tourists or garish swimming trunks. According to Brasilia University's Instituto de Geociencias, the endless curves are all caused by something known as fluvial abrasion, where the pressure of sand and continuously flowing water over several millennia has carved out the cups, bowls and smooth lines that you see today. And they are carving it out still – so it is, in effect, a constantly evolving sculpture.

There's a distinctly lunar feel to the entire landscape, hence the name Vale da Lua. Visitors can walk across the rocks, bathe in the pools and wade down many of the water courses. (Except during heavy rain, when flash flooding makes proceedings very risky indeed.) But most amazing of all are the quartz crystals embedded within the rocks. Thanks to these, some visitors report feeling an added energy and healing power.

● **VALE DA LUA** is on private property, 4km (3 miles) southeast of São Jorge village. The final approach is on foot. Make sure to review current travel advisories before planning a trip.

FERROWHITE

I tried to get on the bus, but all the kiosks around the main square were closed. It was a Sunday, a quiet late-spring afternoon in Bahía Blanca, when most people are either finishing their family *asados* (barbecues) or indulging in the siesta that follows.

I hailed a taxi instead. "How much to the port?" I asked. The driver hesitated, naming a price; I nodded, buckling my seatbelt.

"The port is big," he said. "Where do you want to go? The museum?"

"No," I said. "Take me to Ferrowhite." He looked at me: "Ferrowhite? You know it's haunted, right?"

"I heard something about that," I said. We were on a country road now. Bahía Blanca is an important port, but the city isn't close to the water.

"Yes, there are ghosts there, and reports of extraterrestrial activity," he said. "People died there."

Twenty minutes later, the fields turned into a dense grid of tin houses; beyond the streets, huge barges floated in the bay. The driver took a sharp left, pulling on to a bridge. And then just past the grain elevators and a row of abandoned cargo trains, I saw it: Ferrowhite, suddenly looming grand and ghostly, a concrete castle at the water's edge.

The power plant was built by Italian immigrants in the 1930s. It's true that it was never a safe place to work: this was the site of a series of gruesome deaths, and the plant was abandoned before it was finally dismantled in 1997. Today, a small museum and cultural centre occupy the entryway, but most of the massive building sits empty. There's no one to stop you from walking around it, even climbing inside the periphery of its ruins.

It's a fascinating and vaguely frightening sight, even if you don't believe in ghosts. There were still hours of daylight left, but no other people around. Before I got out of the taxi, I asked the driver, "Can you come back for me in an hour?" –*BRIDGET GLEESON*

★ THE MUSEUM IS open daily; buses run from Bahía Blanca, or you can hire a taxi.

EXQUISITELY PRESERVED CORPSES

Human bodies can be preserved for millennia through deliberate embalming or chance environmental conditions, and these time-trapped corpses give us rare insights into ancient societies. Surprisingly enough, standing in front of a mummified body isn't nightmare fuel: it can even be an act of solemn meditation, forcing you to contemplate the value of life as you stare down its inevitable end.

TEHRAN, IRAN

1. SALT MEN

Mummies, from saints to serial killers, can be popular tourist attractions. Tehran's National Museum exhibits some of the most unusually preserved cadavers, found in the Chehrabad salt mines. Most famed is 3rd-century Zanjan Salt Man, whose bearded head and leg (still clad in a leather boot) have been conserved by the salty conditions.

NUUK, GREENLAND

2. QILAKITSOQ MUMMIES

Dry, Arctic winds preserved the oldest mummies in Greenland. The most unnerving of these 500-year-old Inuit (held at the National Museum) is the doll-like corpse of a six-month-old baby, buried alive with his mother.

EXQUISITELY PRESERVED CORPSES

GORNO-ALTAYSK, RUSSIA

3. UKOK PRINCESS

This Siberian 'ice princess' in the National Museum is adorned with detailed tattoos, from her shoulders to her wrists – and they look surprisingly modern, considering she died 2500 years ago.

COQUEZA, BOLIVIA

4. CEMENTERIO DE CHULLPAS

With knees pulled up to their chins, some still wearing hooded cloaks, seven mummies sit watchfully in a cave on the flanks of Volcán Tunupa. The cave sheltered them from wind and light, keeping them intact. Surrounded by bowls and tools, they're an eerie diorama of pre-Columbian life.

GUANAJUATO, MEXICO

5. GUANAJUATO MUMMIES

More than 100 mummies line the Museo de las Momias, from cholera victims to women buried alive. Creepiest of all is the room of babies dressed as saints to ease their passage to the afterlife.

BOLZANO, ITALY

6. ICEMAN ÖTZI

The grandfather of European mummies, this leathery Tyrolean – preserved in a glacier since 3300 BCE – is older than Stonehenge. Named after the Ötztal Alps where he was found, Ötzi is thought to have been murdered; he now resides in Bolzano's archaeology museum.

SALTA, ARGENTINA

7. LLULLAILLACO CHILDREN

Offered as sacrifices to mediate between gods and the living, the eerily well-preserved Inca children at Salta's Museum of High Altitude Archaeology met their end on top of Llullaillaco volcano on the border between Argentina and Chile.

SIENA, ITALY

8. ST CATHERINE OF SIENA

Framed by a Gothic-style silver reliquary within the Basilica Cateriniana di San Domenico, the head of St Catherine of Siena was smuggled back to her hometown after her death in 1380. Her thumb is also displayed.

PALERMO, ITALY

9. PALERMO'S SLEEPING BEAUTY

The perfectly embalmed body of Rosalia Lombardo, who died of pneumonia in 1920, is on display here. She's one of the youngest corpses in the Catacombe dei Cappuccini.

VARBERG, SWEDEN

10. BOCKSTEN MAN

Dug from a swamp in 1936 (he'd been skewered with an oak spear), the skeletal form of medieval Bocksten Man was discovered in 1936, still sporting strawberry blond hair. The Halland Museum holds his remains and some handsome reconstructions.

CAMINO DE LA MUERTE

The mountain road twists and turns for 64km (40 miles), a ribbon of gravel dwarfed by Bolivia's giant peaks and cliffs. In parts, it's only 3m (10ft) wide – a steep 3500m (11,500ft) drop on one side, potential rockfall on the other – and getting to the end safely requires outstanding driving skills (and a quick prayer wouldn't hurt).

But the road between sprawling La Paz and the subtropical Yungas region is not just a test of nerve; it also traces a brutal chapter of South American history. During the bloody Chaco War (1932–5), when Paraguay and Bolivia battled for control of the oil-rich Gran Chaco region, the La Paz–Yungas road was dynamite-blasted into the pass by Paraguayan prisoners in miserable conditions.

After the war ended and traffic increased, small white crosses began to sprout by the roadside. It became known as the Camino de la Muerte (the Road of Death), as fatalities increased to hundreds per year, particularly during sudden storms. A high-casualty bus accident in 1983 cemented the road's perilous reputation.

When a two-lane highway, Rte 3, was completed in 2007, locals breathed a sigh of relief, and use of the white-knuckle road dropped. With less pollution from cars, locals now notice birdlife flourishing along the Road of Death, and a new species: thrill-seeking tourists. Mountain bikers make special trips here to navigate the tight bends and watch the cloud forests and jagged peaks fly by... do look down.

● **IF YOU'RE REALLY,** really sure you want to experience something called the 'Death Road', book a guided mountain-bike ride with companies such as Gravity Bolivia; excursions start in La Paz. Make sure to review current travel advisories before planning a trip.

Q'ESWACHAKA ROPE BRIDGE

Commonly used by the Inca 600 or so years ago, the Q'eswachaka is the last remaining example of a handwoven bridge. Spanning almost 36m (118ft), and hanging high above the roaring Apurímac River, the bridge is made of braided rope called *q'oya*, crafted using local *ichu* grass. The Q'eswachaka is renewed each June as a symbolic link to the past by four local Quechua communities, who convene in nearby Quehue. The thin *q'oya* ropes made by locals are collected and braided into thicker, stronger ropes by *chakarauwaq* (engineers). They then let the old bridge fall. The new Q'eswachaka is celebrated by giving thanks to the *apus* (mountain spirits), with music and traditional food.

● **IF YOU WANT** to cross the bridge, visit in July or August, when it's new and strong. Make sure to review current travel advisories before planning a trip.

'COLOSO' BY DOMA COLLECTIVE

Electrical towers can't catch a break – we rely on them to run our modern, digital-first lives, but shun these essential towers as eyesores. Around the world, though, artists are honouring these steel giants by transforming them into flamboyant works of art. In Buenos Aires, artist collective Doma turned one 45m/148ft-high pylon into a robotic figure. *Coloso*, the group's entry at Tecnópolis 2012 – a popular art, technology and science fair – comes alive in neon colours, complete with an animated face and a beating heart. Thanks to a sophisticated lighting system, the robot exhibits a range of moods: sometimes he winks and his heart seems to grow larger, other times his smile is practically demonic.

Transmission towers continue to spark artistic inspiration. Art students in Hattingen, Germany, beautified one with colourful panels, while in Újhartyán, Hungary, twin pylons shaped like grinning court jesters overlook the M5 motorway – all to make the mundane truly magical.

● **SEE COLOSO AT** Tecnópolis in the suburb of Vicente López; frequent trains run from Buenos Aires' Retiro station.

PUNTA PITE

A coastal walkway unlike any other, a private park cared for by those living in its midst, or an art project that got entirely out of control? Call it whatever you want – Punta Pite is a mesmerising patch of Chile's central coast that shows how art can surrender to nature. This 11-hectare (27-acre) development between the beach towns of Zapallar and Papudo was the brainchild of landscape architect Teresa Moller. Her designs took a headland jutting out into the Pacific Ocean and transformed it into a stroller's dreamland, with narrow passageways and carefully crafted vistas.

A 1.5km (0.9 mile) route winds along the coast from a pebble beach to natural swimming holes where one can safely enter the sea. The path then climbs upwards along stone staircases (with no railings) to a clifftop lookout, where sculptures by artist Gerardo Aristía are tucked within a patch of cypress trees. Moller employed 40 stonemasons to build the paths at Punta Pite out of hand-cut granite, the same material as the cliffs themselves. The goal was to create an organic mixture of coastal walkways that didn't disturb the landscape, but rather challenged perceptions of it while heightening one's awareness of the natural surroundings. The end result is a humble, yet powerful, spatial experience for visitors to this stretch of the Chilean coast.

● **FREE AND OPEN** to the public, Punta Pite is an easy 3km (1.9 mile) walk (or drive) from the beach town of Papudo.

ROCK PAINTINGS OF PARQUE NACIONAL DA SERRA DA CAPIVARA

With its remarkable red-stone arches and a riot of greenery erupting from between the cliffs, the 1300-sq-km (502-sq-mile) Parque Nacional da Serra da Capivara is a UNESCO World Heritage Site famous for some 40,000 prehistoric rock paintings – the densest concentration of rock art on Earth. Of the 300 or so archaeological sites, most consist of rock paintings dating back to 30,000–50,000 BCE. This is the oldest and most compelling evidence of human presence in the Americas, which predates other finds by about 30,000 years.

Visitors make their way around the 170 or so sites open to the public using the four main driving circuits, walking trails and wooden walkways. The art on rock walls and inside stony shelters sheds light on the lives of some of South America's earliest inhabitants. Many images depict animals, and scenes of hunting, celebration, dancing and sex. The people who made them are believed to have been hunter-gatherers, followed by more sophisticated ceramic-crafting agricultural societies.

Some of the most important sites include the Boqueirão da Pedra Furada, with its 50,000-year-old remains of ancient hearths, illuminated at night. Lucky visitors may spot some of the park's abundant yet shy wildlife – from leopards and wildcats to armadillos.

• **A MANDATORY LOCAL** guide can be arranged at most lodgings in São Raimundo Nonato, 35km (22 miles) away. Make sure to review current travel advisories before planning a trip.

CORDILLERA, PERU

SOMBRERO OF CELENDÍN

In the highlands of the verdant Cordillera Central in northern Peru, the town of Celendín is known for its handcrafted straw hats. So much so, in fact, that the gazebo in Parque del Sombrero on the southern approach to town has been transformed to look like a giant version of just such a hat, with people congregating in the ample shade offered by its wide brim. The iconic high-topped straw hats themselves are a work of true artisanship; they are made using *toquilla* straw (also used in the making of Ecuador's world-famous Panama hats), with individual strands woven and tightened by local craftspeople. A bespoke hat takes anything from a few weeks to months to be crafted.

• **CELENDÍN IS ABOUT** 100km (62 miles) northeast of Cajamarca; buses connect the two. Make sure to review current travel advisories before planning a trip.

ANTARCTICA

DECEPTION ISLAND

Deception Island sparkles in the remote South Shetland Islands archipelago, which skims the northern edge of the Antarctic Peninsula. Deceptive in more ways than one, its secret harbour is ensconced in the caldera of a 'restless' volcano, always threatening to blow. Sail through the narrow opening to enter the horse-shoe-shaped bay surrounded by black-sand beaches and slopes of ash-covered snow and ice, which hide chinstrap penguin rookeries. After spying on the cacophonous breeding birds, sleuth through the island's industrial archaeology at its abandoned whaling station, partially destroyed by an eruption-induced mudflow and flood. And, naturally, don't forget to pack your swimsuit, since you can take a plunge into the island's heated geothermal currents for the ultimate polar adventure.

• **REACH DECEPTION ISLAND** on an Antarctic cruise departing from Argentina.

CUEVA DEL MILODÓN

There are many reasons for making the extraordinary effort required to get to this part of Patagonia. Heading to a cave where the skin and fur of a giant sloth was found may not, on first inspection, be one of them. But, given that a piece of this very skin was the thing that inspired Bruce Chatwin's own famous Patagonian journey, surely what's good enough for one of the world's greatest travellers is a secret worth exploring?

Your voyage here will be satisfyingly difficult: either a bumpy flight, a long bus trip or a stomach-churning ferry ride via dramatic fjordland to the north, bringing you to Puerto Natales, the nearest town.

Though the replica mylodon at the entrance is a decidedly modern intervention, the secret here is the window into the everyday lives of the early humans who hunted and lived in (and near) these caves as early as 6000 BCE. There are several caves here, as well as unusual rock formations and a lookout over the end-of-the-world scenery of Patagonia, where you can contemplate their precarious existence. Your mind may also wander from the fate of the mylodon, whose remains were discovered here, to other exotic wildlife found at the cave – including, in a marvellous quirk of nomenclature, the Smilodon sabre-toothed cat.

● **THE CAVE IS** close to the main road from Puerto Natales into Parque Nacional Torres del Paine, and is usually visited as part of the journey there.

CATATUMBO LIGHTNING

Lightning *does* strike twice at Lake Maracaibo. In fact, it pummels the same spots many times over: each quarter-kilometre of this northwestern Venezuela region is struck by up to 250 bolts of lightning every year.

The boglands where the Catatumbo River melts into 36-million-year-old Lake Maracaibo endure the most frequent lightning strikes on the planet. The winds chase moist, warm air from the lake to meet cool air from the Andes. These colliding currents brew gigantic cumulonimbus clouds, which spread out against the heavens until their electrical charges build and build, discharging in lightning that rips through the sky.

Lake Maracaibo's night skies glow for up to 300 days in the year. For visitors, it's a spectacular light show, where spears of lightning illuminate the clouds a dusky pink with every flash. For locals, it's nothing new: just mood lightning that has accompanied their nights for millennia.

Then and now, the lake is a life force. Stilt-houses built at its edge prompted Italian explorer Amerigo Vespucci to dub the region Veneziola (Little Venice) in 1499, which later became 'Venezuela'. Navigators have long used these dazzling skies like a lighthouse, but for local fishers, lightning poses a serious risk, killing as many as three people per year. Researchers are busily masterminding better ways to detect gathering storms so locals can avoid the lightning, even as visitors arrive to chase it.

* **AT THE TIME** of writing, travel was not advised to Venezuela.

☀ PHOTO CREDITS

Cover and interior illustrations by Lauren Crow

5: (tl) Jason deCaires Taylor (sculptor), (tr) Damien Tachoires/500px, (br) Frazer Lockhart/Shutterstock, (bl) sivarock/Getty Images; 6: chris piason/Shutterstock; 9: (l) Helmut Wienerroither via Adunni Olorisha Trust/Adunni Osun Foundation, (r) Harry Hook/Getty Images; 11: Matteo Bertolino; 12: DorSteffen/Shutterstock; 13: (l) JPRichard/Shutterstock, (r) Richard van der Spuy/Shutterstock; 15: Cezary Wojtkowski/Shutterstock; 16: (tl) MattL_Images/Shutterstock, (tr) Nadeem A. Khan/Shutterstock, (br) studioanghifoto/Shutterstock, (bl) MartiBstock Shutterstock; 18: Arterra/Getty Images; 19: imageBROKER/Mara Brandl/Getty Images; 20: Kirill Trubitsyn/Shutterstock; 21: DeAgostini/Getty Images; 22: Grobler du Preez/Shutterstock; 23: Curioso.Photography/Shutterstock; 24: Tavarius/Shutterstock; 27: Maurizio De Mattei/Shutterstock; 28: Rostasedlacek/Shutterstock; 29: Danita Delimont/Shutterstock; 30: Anadolu/Getty Images; 31: Helder Almeida/Shutterstock; 33: Alexey Kharitonov/Shutterstock; 35: chasdesign/Shutterstock; 36: (tl) marcobriviophoto.com/Shutterstock, (tr) Daniel Prudek/Shutterstock, (br) Peter Seaward for Lonely Planet, (bl) Electric Egg/Shutterstock; 38: Philip Lee Harvey for Lonely Planet; 39: Robert Harding Video; 40: Olympia de Maismont/Getty Images; 42: tvcuong8892/Shutterstock; 44: Peter Stuckings/Shutterstock; 45: Meklay Yotkhamsay/Shutterstock; 46: Johannes Zielcke/Shutterstock; 47: totogo1015/Shutterstock; 48: Matt Munro for Lonely Planet; 50: Thongchai.S/Shutterstock; 51: Sofiaworld/Shutterstock; 52: Kylie Nicholson/Shutterstock; 53: (r) Chris McGrath/Getty Images, (l) Taiwan Tourism Administration; 54: SM Rafiq Photography/Getty Images; 55: Mhao Studio/Shutterstock; 57: shushonok/Shutterstock; 59: Intellistudies/Shutterstock; 60: (tl) n.tati.m/Shutterstock, (tr) Emmanuel Rulona/Shutterstock, (br) Denis Moskvinov/Shutterstock, (bl) Haobo Wang/Shutterstock; 62: otorongo/Shutterstock; 63: BFA/Alamy; 64: Morten Falch Sortland/Getty Images; 66: MDV Edwards/Shutterstock; 67: saeedreza/Shutterstock; 68: Marser/Getty Images; 69: (r) Kinstory/Shutterstock, (l) James Talalay/Alamy; 70: by Alla/Shutterstock; 71: Poliorketes/Shutterstock; 72: akimov konstantin/Shutterstock; 75: lemaret pierrick/Shutterstock; 77: James Pham/Lonely Planet; 78: (r) mapman/Shutterstock, (l) dani daniar/Shutterstock; 79: Temir Shintemirov/Shutterstock; 80: Cavan-Images/Shutterstock; 82: flocu/Shutterstock; 83: liamwood_shots/Shutterstock; 84: Iwanami Photos/Shutterstock; 85: alexkoral/Shutterstock; 87: Torsten Pursche/Shutterstock; 88: (tl) imageBROKER/Alamy, (tr) worldswildlifewonders/Shutterstock, (br) Ryan M. Bolton/Shutterstock, (bl) Luca Diehl/Shutterstock; 91: Jianhua Qiu/500px; 92: SeanPavonePhoto/Getty Images; 93: georgeclerk/Getty Images; 94: (r) GaudiLab/Shutterstock, (l) Jarel Remick/500px; 95: Rio Adera/Shutterstock; 96: Dawn Minkow/Shutterstock; 98: Sidney van den Boogaard/Shutterstock; 99: (l) takepicsforfun/Shutterstock, (r) Jonathan Stokes for Lonely Planet; 100: Charlene Manet/Shutterstock; 102: (l) Rini Kools/Getty Images, (r) Vera Larina/Shutterstock; 103: Rosanne Tackaberry/Alamy; 105: Danita Delimont/Alamy; 106: dpa picture alliance/Alamy; 109: Alizada Studios/Shutterstock; 110: (tl) myphotobank.com.au/Shutterstock, Paul Kelly (artist), (tr) Willowtreehouse/Shutterstock, Gary Dutallis (architect), (br) Alizada Studios/Shutterstock, Ben van Zetten (artist), (bl) Paul Harding 00/Shutterstock, Kevin Thomas (artist); 112: ian woolcock/Shutterstock; 113: MarcelStrelow/Getty Images; 114: Jim Pozarik/Getty Images; 116: (l) Wendell Teodoro/Getty Images, (r) Pvince73/Shutterstock; 118: Nicram Sabod/Shutterstock; 121: Venca11/Shutterstock; 122: jefferyhamstock/Shutterstock; 123: alvarobueno/Shutterstock; 124: maloff/Shutterstock; 125: Jason Edwards/Getty Images; 129: Janice Chen/Shutterstock; 130: (tl) Belikova Oksana/Shutterstock, (tr) zzz555zzz/Shutterstock, (br) Robert Harding Video/Shutterstock, (bl) Carol Polich for Lonely Planet; 132: Adam Fawcett via DCCEEW; 133: LyndonOK/Shutterstock; 135: robert mcgillivray/Shutterstock; 136: (l) Darkydoors/Shutterstock, (r) superjoseph/Shutterstock; 137: RobNaw/Shutterstock; 138: Creative Travel Projects/Shutterstock; 140: (l) Engel Ching/Shutterstock, (r)

PeterDKent/Shutterstock, Andy Scott (artist); **141:** Chalie Chulapornsiri/Shutterstock; **143:** Andre Chet/Shutterstock; **145:** (r) Patrick Verhoef/Shutterstock, (l) Justin Foulkes for Lonely Planet; **147:** Henry Nicholls/Getty Images; **148:** (tl) Alex_Mastro/Shutterstock, (tr) Baloncici/Shutterstock, (br) Imars/Alamy, (bl) Simon Turner/Alamy; **150:** weniliou/Shutterstock; **151:** 365 Focus Photography/Shutterstock; **153:** Kirill Skorobogatko/Shutterstock; **154:** Kamil Kwiatkowski/Shutterstock; **155:** (r) anastas_styles/Shutterstock, (l) Pasotteo/Shutterstock; **156:** borzywoj/Shutterstock; **157:** goran_safarek/Shutterstock; **158:** AJSTUDIO Photography/Shutterstock; **161:** Florin P/Alamy; **163:** (r) Yevgen Belich/Shutterstock, Neringa Museums, Hill of Witches sculptures, ;**165:** Julen Arabaolaza/Shutterstock; **166:** Alex Skelly/Getty Images; **168:** BearFotos/Shutterstock; **169:** MNStudio/Shutterstock; **170:** ginger_polina_bublik/Shutterstock; **171:** Arterra Picture Library/Alamy; **173:** alexemanuel/Getty Images; **174:** (tl) Olga Gavrilova/Shutterstock, (tr) lkpro/Shutterstock, (br) AZCat/Shutterstock, (bl) lu_sea/Shutterstock; **177:** (r) Koutas/Shutterstock, (l) Kisa_Markiza/iStock; **178:** (r) Cimermane/Shutterstock, (l) TeleMakro Fotografie/Alamy; **179:** Denis Prezat/Getty Images; **181:** (r) Marek M/Shutterstock, (l) Alberto Loyo/Shutterstock; **182:** Aleph/Getty Images; **183:** (t) Joe McUbed/Shutterstock, (b) Agorca/Shutterstock; **184:** gorsh13/Getty Images; **185:** Julian Worker/Shutterstock; **186:** Carol Mellema/Shutterstock; **189:** Keith Levit/Shutterstock; **190:** Joseph Holoien/Shutterstock; **191:** Art of roaming/Shutterstock; **192:** Vezzani Photography/Shutterstock; **194:** Alex Pix/Shutterstock; **195:** (l) christianthiel.net/Shutterstock, (r) Darryl Brooks/Shutterstock; **196:** Marisol Rios Campuzano/Shutterstock; **199:** Matt Munro for Lonely Planet; **200:** (tl) Alexandre.Rosa/Shutterstock, (tr) Glenn Taylor/Shutterstock, (br) Ned Snowman/Shutterstock, (bl) Franck Photos/Alamy; **203:** Wirestock Creators/Shutterstock; **205:** (r) ferrantraite/Getty Images, (l) NPC Collectiom/Alamy; **206:** (t) timothy mattimore/iStock, (b) Bryan Neuswanger/Shutterstock; **207:** Photo Spirit/Shutterstock; **208:** Mark Skerbinek/Getty Images; **209:** Raul Luna/Shutterstock; **210:** David Buzzard/Alamy; **212:** Nick 1L/Shutterstock; **215:** Ian Dewar Photography/Shutterstock; **216:** Abbie Warnock-Matthews/Shutterstock; **217:** Inspired By Maps/Shutterstock; **218:** EWY Media/Shutterstock; **220:** Jon Arnold Images Ltd/Alamy; **223:** Justin Foulkes for Lonely Planet; **224:** christopher babcock/Shutterstock; **225:** steflas/Shutterstock; **226:** (t) Bill45/Shutterstock, (b) iMediaPictures/Shutterstock; **229:** travellinglight/Alamy, Bret Thurston (architect); **230:** (tl) Phyllis Madonna/Newsmakers/Getty Images, (tr) EvrenKalinbacak/Shutterstock, (br) May-lin Joe/Getty Images, (bl) Colin Bourne/Shutterstock; **232:** Galyna Andrushko/Shutterstock; **235:** Aaron Huey via Salvation Mountain, Inc; **236:** David Whitemyer/Shutterstock; **238:** Javier Trueba/MSF/Science Photo Library; **240:** Dusty Roads/Shutterstock; **241:** ZUMA Press Inc/Alamy; **242:** Jason deCaires Taylor (sculptor); **243:** Jason deCaires Taylor (sculptor); **244:** Davide Savio/Shutterstock; **247:** Alfredo Cerra/Shutterstock; **248:** Tuul and Bruno Morandi/Alamy; **249:** reisegraf.ch/Shutterstock; **250:** Jorge Ivan Vasquez C/Shutterstock; **252:** Kamran Ali/Shutterstock; **255:** dragonia98/Shutterstock; **256:** (tl) TTstudio/Shutterstock, (tr) Captured By Lukas/Shutterstock, (br) LuFilu/Shutterstock, (bl) Lina Lobanova/Shutterstock; **258:** Jhampier Giron M/Shutterstock; **260:** Vadim Petrakov/Shutterstock; **262:** Sandro Helmann/Getty Images; **264:** Lucas Barillari Prates/Shutterstock; **266:** Diego Grandi/Shutterstock; **267:** Andres Conema/Alamy; **268:** Vinicius R. Souza/Shutterstock; **271:** vlopesjr/Shutterstock; **272:** Lucas Rachinski/500px; **275:** Ralf Hettler/Getty Images; **277:** Alberto Loyo/Shutterstock; **279:** Fotos593/Shutterstock; **280:** vitormarigo/Shutterstock; **283:** Freedom_wanted/Shutterstock; **284:** imageBROKER.com/Alamy; **286:** (t) filrom/Getty Images, (b) Andrew Clifforth/Shutterstock; **287:** Aleksandar Todorovic/Shutterstock; **288:** 'Coloso' by Doma Collective; **289:** abriendomundo/Shutterstock; **290:** (t) Brazil Photos/Getty Images, (b) Marcos Amend/Shutterstock; **291:** Marcos Amend/Shutterstock; **292:** MB Photography/Getty Images; **293:** Adwo/Shutterstock; **295:** christianpinillo/Shutterstock

SECRET WONDERS OF THE WORLD

July 2026
Published by Lonely Planet Global Limited
CRN: 554153
ISBN: 9781806532926
© Lonely Planet 2026
10 9 8 7 6 5 4 3 2 1 Printed in Malaysia

PUBLISHING DIRECTOR Piers Pickard
EDITORIAL DIRECTOR Becca Hunt
PROJECT EDITOR Margo Rosenbaum
SENIOR EDITOR Robin Barton
ILLUSTRATIONS Lauren Crow
CREATIVE DIRECTION Emily Dubin
ART DIRECTION & DESIGN Taylor Miles Hopkins
TYPESETTER Hillary Caudle
COORDINATING EDITOR Anita Isalska
EDITORS Polly Thomas, Anne Mason, Joanna Cooke, Karyn Noble
PRINT PRODUCTION Nigel Longuet

WRITERS Alex Howard, Alexis Averbuck, Amy Balfour, Amy Karafin, Anita Isalska, Anna Kaminski, Anthony Ham, Bailey Johnson, Brandon Presser, Brendan Sainsbury, Brian Kluepfel, Bridget Gleeson, Carolyn B Heller, Celeste Brash, Craig McLaughlin, Dominic Bliss, Duncan Garwood, Emilie Filou, Etain O'Carroll, Gregor Clark, Helen Ranger, James Bainbridge, James Dorsey, JB Carillet, Joe Bindloss, Jonathan Thompson, Karla Zimmerman, Karyn Noble, Kate Armstrong, Kate Morgan, Kevin Raub, Laura Crawford, Lucy Corne, Luna Soo, Marc di Duca, Mark Johanson, Matt Phillips, Nana Luckham, Pat Yale, Paul Harding, Phillip Tang, Ray Bartlett, Rebecca Warren, Regis St Louis, Steve Fallon, Tamara Sheward, Tom Hall, Tom Masters, Tom O'Malley, Tracy Whitmey, Trent Holden, Virginia Jealous

All rights reserved. No part of this publication may be reproduced, stored in a retrieval system or transmitted in any form by any means, electronic, mechanical, photocopying, recording or otherwise except brief extracts for the purpose of review, without the written permission of the publisher. Lonely Planet and the Lonely Planet logo are trademarks of Lonely Planet and are registered in the US Patent and Trademark Office and in other countries.

Although the author and Lonely Planet have taken all reasonable care in preparing this book, we make no warranty about the accuracy or completeness of its content and, to the maximum extent permitted, disclaim all liability from its use.

STAY IN TOUCH lonelyplanet.com/contact

LONELY PLANET OFFICE
IRELAND
Digital Depot, Roe Lane (off Thomas St),
Digital Hub, Dublin 8, D08 TCV4, Ireland
(EU authorised representative)

Paper in this book is certified against the Forest Stewardship Council™ standards. FSC™ promotes environmentally responsible, socially beneficial and economically viable management of the world's forests.